OXFORD PHILOSOPHICAL MONOGRAPHS

Editorial Committee

THINGS THAT HAPPEN
BECAUSE THEY SHOULD

Things That Happen Because They Should

A Teleological Approach To Action

ROWLAND STOUT

OXFORD UNIVERSITY PRESS

1996

Oxford University Press, Walton Street, Oxford OX2 6DP
Oxford New York
Athens Auckland Bangkok Bogota Bombay
Buenos Aires Calcutta Cape Town Dar es Salaam
Delhi Florence Hong Kong Istanbul Karachi
Kuala Lumpur Madras Madrid Melbourne
Mexico City Nairobi Paris Singapore
Taipei Tokyo Toronto
and associated companies in
Berlin Ibadan

Oxford is a trade mark of Oxford University Press

Published in the United States
by Oxford University Press Inc., New York

British Library Cataloguing in Publication Data
Data available

Library of Congress Cataloging-in-Publication Data
Stout, Rowland.
Things that happen because they should : a teleological approach
to action / Rowland Stout.
(Oxford philosophical monographs)
Includes bibliographical references.
1. Act (Philosophy) 2. Teleology. I. Title. II. Series.
B105.A35S76 1996 128'.4—dc20 96-20124
ISBN 0-19-824063-5

1 3 5 7 9 10 8 6 4 2

Typeset by Best-set Typesetter Ltd., Hong Kong
Printed in Great Britain
on acid-free paper by
Biddles Ltd, Guildford and King's Lynn

To Sarah

PREFACE

WITH much gratitude, I would like to acknowledge the help of the following people, all of whom have read and commented on parts of this book in earlier versions: Bill Child, Sarah Gracie, Jennifer Hornsby, John McDowell, Michael Martin, Alfred Mele, Carolyn Price, Paul Snowdon, David Stout, Ralph Walker, and Tim Williamson. In particular, I would like to thank David Charles who has been a constant source of intellectual and practical support.

In addition, I am very grateful to Oriel College, Oxford, for granting me sabbatical leave for a term to concentrate on writing this book, and to the Department of Traditional and Modern Philosophy in Sydney University for giving me access to their facilities during that time.

It may be worth mentioning that throughout this book I have adopted the use of 'they' as the personal pronoun of indeterminate gender rather than 'he' or 'she'.

R.A.K.S.

CONTENTS

x   *Contents*

Introduction

I think that intentional actions are unique among natural phenomena in that they happen because they should happen. This is not to say that they happen because they ought to *morally*, although perhaps they sometimes do. It is to say that there are ways of *evaluating* actions as rational or irrational, as justified or unjustified; and it is because they are rational or justified, according to such a way of evaluating things, that they happen.

This is a highly controversial thesis; it amounts to saying that value has a causal role to play in nature. It goes against the orthodox view that evaluations are only *projected* on to the world by us; they are not part of the fabric of nature and so cannot themselves make anything happen.

A central way in which actions are evaluated is in terms of what ends they serve—i.e. teleologically. Aristotle had a notion of teleological explanation as explanation of something in terms of what it is for the sake of. According to Aristotle, we explain the presence of teeth in animals teleologically by saying that they are there to enable the animal to eat; we teleologically explain someone going for a walk by saying that they are walking for the sake of their health. Somehow the fact that these things are means to further ends is supposed to explain them.

But this notion of teleological explanation has come to seem scientifically disreputable in the light of the development of mechanistic models of scientific explanation. The progress made in the age of Enlightenment in accounting for things without recourse to God or magic may seem to have eliminated the need for the Aristotelian notion of teleological explanation. According to such mechanistic models, we properly explain one thing by describing the way the world is at an earlier time in sufficient detail that given certain basic laws of nature that thing is seen to have been inevitable. If the fact that something was the best means to achieve a particular end had a key role in such an explanation, it could only be in virtue of the holding of some basic teleological law of nature—like the law that things will turn out for the best in the end. The prospect of there being such a law seems to us now to be an absurdly optimistic fantasy.

Even if actual teleology is not considered to have any role in proper explanations of things, modern philosophers are still moved by the *apparent* role of teleology in our thinking about evolution and action. These philosophers maintain some role for means-end sensitivity in explanation, but in a more indirect way than Aristotle would have it. According to this approach, the evolutionary explanation of why we have teeth now is not quite supposed to be that having teeth serves a purpose for us. Rather, it is that in the past having teeth served a purpose for some of our ancestors. The means-end part of this explanation is embedded in a historical fact; the fact that having teeth enabled some of those ancestors to eat things and thereby survive and reproduce. Similarly, in the explanation of action, the explanation of why I go for a walk is not quite supposed to be that my going for a walk serves some purpose for me. Rather, it is that there is some psychological state I am in before going for a walk which *represents* that the walk serves some purpose for me. The means-end part of the explanation is embedded in the content of my prior mental states. In both cases, the teleological part of the explanation is tucked away somewhere safe where it is not itself making anything happen.

I want to defend a much more strongly Aristotelian conception of teleological explanation. I will argue that there is a causal explanation of why we have teeth in terms of the fact that teeth actually serve some purpose for *us*; and that there is a causal explanation of why I go for a walk in terms of the fact that going for a walk actually serves a purpose for me rather than in terms of its simply being represented as serving a purpose. And I will argue that this strongly Aristotelian notion, despite allowing a causal role for value in nature, may fit quite respectably in the company of mechanistic explanations of things in terms of previous states of affairs.

In the philosophy of action, this Aristotelian claim is located in a very strong externalism about the *reasons* for action. According to this strong externalism, the reason for my going for a walk is the *fact* that walking is good for the health. Although this may sound fine at first, it is easy to come to think that it is too strong a claim and that the real and immediate explanation for my going for a walk should be my *belief* that walking is good for the health rather than the fact that it is. When your beliefs are false, you still act according to them rather than according to the facts; so it looks as if your actions must be directly causally sensitive to beliefs not facts.

For this reason, few philosophers nowadays would hold on to the claim that external facts about means serving ends should figure in the most immediate explanations of people's actions. The orthodox view is that any explanation of action will be mediated by reference to a person's beliefs and intentions (or desires). In this book I go against this orthodoxy and argue that it is possible to explain people's behaviour teleologically in terms of the facts without making any reference at all to their beliefs and intentions. This is the central controversial claim of the book.

One strategy that some philosophers have had for maintaining a strongly Aristotelian conception of teleological explanation is to deny that such explanations of action are *causal*, or at any rate to deny that it is the external reasons that are doing the causal work. They argue that explaining something involves making it intelligible; and that making something intelligible may involve doing other things than telling a story about what made it happen.

This is not my strategy. I argue that teleological explanations are causal. Moreover I argue for a broadly realist conception of causal explanation. I urge that behind correct causal explanations should be causal processes which are grounded in some real underlying nature; a correct explanation of something should describe a process which actually results in that thing. My claim is that actions are the immediate results of causal processes which are sensitive to actual (external) means-end considerations.

This claim about the explanation of action may be exploited in an account of what actions are. I call this account the Teleological Theory of Action. According to this theory, activity constitutes intentional action in virtue of being causally explainable in terms of a teleological justification of it.

I think that my account of processes provides the resources to solve one of the most awkward problems faced by any causal theory of action, including my Teleological Theory. This is the problem of deviant causal chains; and it besets causal theories of perception, knowledge, reference, etc., as well as causal theories of action. According to the Teleological Theory of Action, if some activity is causally explainable in terms of something which teleologically justifies it, then it constitutes intentional action. The problem arises if the causal path to the activity is deviant and involves quite fortuitous (though, at some level, causally explicable) connections. If some activity is caused in such a way, then it does *not* constitute intentional action.

What has gone wrong in such cases is that activity is caused by the right sort of thing but in the wrong sort of way—i.e. by the wrong sort of process. So deviant causal chains involve the right cause but the wrong causal process. If the theory of action is framed in terms of causal processes rather than just in terms of causes, there is some prospect that deviant cases can be ruled out.

This suggests that the notion of a causal process should probably be taken much more seriously by philosophers. I argue that it cannot be reduced to the notion of an event. Whereas events extend over time and have temporal parts, processes persist through time and do not have temporal parts. I claim that processes are real entities of quite a different and perhaps more basic sort from events. They are not just series of events, but substantial continuants in their own right.

This is one respect in which my account of action differs from that of Davidson. I am following Davidson exactly in the way he sets up the problem of deviant causal chains. What is happening in deviant cases is that activity is caused by the right sort of thing but in the wrong sort of way. What Davidson famously despaired of spelling out was 'the way in which attitudes must cause actions if they are to rationalize the action' (1980: 79). According to my diagnosis, this despair is only appropriate given Davidson's insistence that the primitive causal relation is a relation between events. If the primitive causal relation is a relation between a process and a result, then there is no such cause for concern.

My Teleological Theory of Action is in other ways very similar to Davidson's account, although he might balk at describing it as a *theory* of action. He writes that 'if an event is an action, then under some description(s) . . . it is intentional' (1980: 61). And in another article he claims that 'an action is performed with a certain intention if it is caused in the right way by attitudes and beliefs that rationalize it' (1980: 87). So he is claiming that an event is an action if it is causally explained in the right sort of way by a justification of it in terms of the appropriate attitudes and beliefs.

Like Davidson, I claim that an event constitutes an action in virtue of being explained in terms of a justification of it. What makes my Teleological Theory of Action different from Davidson's account is that I do not spell out this justification in terms of attitudes and beliefs. I claim that the appropriate notion of justification can be spelt out without mentioning beliefs and intentions at all.

This opens up the way for me to provide a behaviourist account of beliefs and intentions. It is undeniable that a person has only acted intentionally if they have some appropriate beliefs and intentions. But this undeniable truth need not be taken to be part of one's theory of *action*, as Davidson takes it. Instead, it may be taken to be part of one's theory of *mind*. Given an account of what it is to act intentionally which does not depend on this undeniable truth, this undeniable truth may be used to provide an account of what it is to have beliefs and intentions.

I call this account Teleological Behaviourism. The teleological notion of justification is an ineliminable part of the account. In this respect I share Davidson's anti-reductionism. One cannot give an account of how to interpret someone's behaviour as intentional action without making use of the notion of rationality (or justification). Assuming, with Davidson, that no complete specification of rationality can be given, then no completely specified account of beliefs and intentions can be given either.

It is still appropriate to call my account behaviourist, however. Although I do not reduce mental notions to non-intentional, non-normative notions, I do reduce mental notions to non-mental notions. I give an account of what it is for a subject to believe something or to intend to achieve something which, although it uses the notion of justification, makes no reference to any of the subject's mental states.

The Possibility of Externalist Explanation of Action

A. TELEOLOGICAL EXPLANATION OF ACTION

One way we have of explaining things is to say that they happen because they should happen. Arriving late for school one morning two children miss the school assembly and are asked to explain why. When the first mumbles something about the buses being late, the teacher tells him that this is no *justification* at all, but merely an *excuse*. He is left floundering. The teacher is not accusing him of lying, but instead of some moral shortcoming in the nature of his explanation. But what is wrong with an excuse? What else can be required?

Then it is his friend's turn to explain herself. She says that she has missed assembly because her asthma was particularly bad, and it would have been exacerbated by the crush of bodies in the hall. This is a more impressive explanation. Whereas the explanation of the first student has put him in the role of a passive hostage to fortune, her's has put her in the role of an *agent*. She has not merely explained her missing of assembly, she has justified it, and by doing so has somehow put *herself* in the picture.

This story suggests the thought that it is only by being able to explain one's activity in terms of a practical justification like this that one can claim to be a real agent at all. This book aims to develop this thought into a fully blown theory of agency. The theory I want to develop is not just a theory of action; it is also an account of those intentional mental states and processes, such as believing and intending, which are essential to agency. It is an account of these things entirely in terms of explanations and potential explanations of activity by practical justifications.

Such a theory must be defended against an alternative and more orthodox philosophical approach, which takes the relation between practical justification and the intentional mental states essential for agency to be the other way round. Rather than claiming, as I will, that the asthmatic student's agency depends on her activity being explainable in terms of a practical justification, it is more usual to claim that the practical justification of her activity is only available in virtue of the fact that she is an agent with beliefs and desires. According to this alternative approach, the practical justification of her activity must be in terms of her *desire* not to exacerbate her asthma and her *belief* that going to assembly would exacerbate her asthma. According to my approach, the practical justification of her activity may be entirely in terms of external facts with no need to mention beliefs and desires.

I will approach this fully blown theory of agency by considering first what seems to be a much less controversial theory concerning *action*. This is the theory that it is only in virtue of activity being explainable in terms of a practical justification that it constitutes intentional action. It is clear that according to the first student's story, his missing of assembly is not an intentional action; whereas, according to the second student's story, her's is. Can this difference be put down entirely to the fact that her activity is explainable in terms of a practical justification and his is not?

I will define explanation in terms of a practical justification (whatever that is) as *teleological explanation*. At this stage, this just serves as a handy stipulation. Later I will discuss whether this is the best way to define teleological explanation. But, given this definition, I can now label the claim under discussion as the Teleological Theory of Action.

> The Teleological Theory of Action: Activity constitutes intentional action in virtue of being explainable in terms of a practical justification of it.

An initial worry with this concerns the role of explanation in the theory. Isn't an explanation of a phenomenon quite incidental to the phenomenon? The explanation happens afterwards if at all, and depends on various social conditions which are irrelevant to the nature of the thing being explained. If some activity instantaneously brought about the end of the world no one would be around to explain it, but it would be no less of an action for that.

This worry is too strongly expressed since the claim is not that activity constitutes intentional action in virtue of being *explained* in a certain way, but that it constitutes intentional action in virtue of being *explainable* in a certain way. Even so, there is something rather indirect about using explanation in the account at all. To say that something is explainable is to say that some preconditions of its being explained are satisfied. These preconditions are likely to involve the right sort of causal relation holding. So, in the end, the account could be formulated in terms of this causal relation, making no mention of explanation. In the mean time, however, it does no harm to think of action in terms of explanation, and it certainly enables one to connect with more of the philosophical literature on the subject.

Another worry about the Teleological Theory of Action concerns the fact that it claims to be a theory of *intentional* action. If not all action is intentional, then an account of agency should start with the more general notion of action and then work up to intentional action. There seems to be something rather suspicious about making the apparently *compound* notion of intentional action the basic notion in an account of agency. If all action is intentional, then the honest way to frame the Teleological Theory of Action is as an account of action and not as an account of intentional action.

O'Shaughnessy, in his treatment of action discusses what he calls sub-intentional acts (1980: vol. ii, ch. 10). He gives the example of moving one's tongue around one's mouth without thinking about it. He claims that in such cases the movement is not intended and moreover that 'the faculty of reason is completely by-passed' (1980: ii. 61). Yet, he claims that when I become aware of the movement of my tongue, 'I become aware, not merely of *a movement* of my tongue, but of a movement that *I have executed*. But more, I become aware of *an activity of moving* that is being performed by me. I notice an *act-event*' (1980: ii. 60).

If the possibility of this type of unconscious tongue-moving is to stand as a counter-example to the Teleological Theory of Action, the following claims are needed:

1. Unconsciously moving one's tongue is an action.
2. In unconsciously moving one's tongue, the faculty of reason is completely bypassed.
3. When something is explainable in terms of a practical justification, that just is the engagement of the faculty of reason.

I do not want to deny the third claim, but one or both of the first two claims can be questioned.

I feel a strong intuitive inclination to deny that the unconscious movement of my tongue is something that I make happen or that I execute. In general, one cannot rely on the inference from a piece of activity being something I do to that activity being something I make happen or execute. To take a clearer example, consider someone who is asleep and breathing. Breathing is something the sleeping person does, that is for sure. But it is not something they *make happen*. To mark this distinction, we might say that breathing is an *activity* of the sleeping person, but not an *action*.[1] Since the word 'action' is sometimes used without carrying this implication of the agent making something happen, we might choose to mark this distinction even more clearly by talking of intentional action. This phrase can be taken as a whole and need not commit us to the possibility of actions not being intentional.

If it is wrong to describe unconsciously moving one's tongue as something that one makes happen or that one executes as well as something that one does, then I think it is equally wrong to describe it as a sub-intentional act. Unfortunately, O'Shaughnessy's intuitions about what to say about unconsciously moving one's tongue are quite different from mine. He claims that it *is* something that the agent makes happen. Since intuitions seem to be sliding here, how are we to get a grip on the notion of action?

One way might be to insist that actions must involve that which is essential to the agency of the person acting. According to O'Shaughnessy's theory, what makes someone an agent is that they have a will—that they are capable of striving. According to my approach, what makes someone an agent is that their activity is explainable by practical justifications. These different approaches

---

[1] The word 'act' is used by O'Shaughnessy interchangeably with the word 'action'.

to agency lead to different conceptions of what an action is—striving, according to O'Shaughnessy, and teleologically explainable activity, according to me.

This suggests that the Teleological Theory of Action may not be much less controversial after all than the teleological account of agency which this whole book is intended to develop. O'Shaughnessy's example of an unconsciously moving tongue does not provide a clear counter-example to the Teleological Theory of Action, since it depends on intuitions about what actions are that are rooted in a contentious account of agency, as well as on his arguments that the movement of the tongue is a striving. But equally, I have no quick way to argue that such a movement is not an action. The claim that it is not an action seems to depend on the viability of the teleological approach to agency.

Whatever one's approach to agency, the example is a problematic one. It seems to be a borderline case between mere activity and action. Even if the movement is not something the agent makes happen, it is closely connected to the agency of the agent. The movement is something the agent *could* make happen or not happen, and as such is within the control and responsibility of the agent, even when the agent is not in fact controlling it. The activity is *within* the agency of the agent even if it is not the result of that agency. It is unclear in such cases whether the faculty of reason is completely bypassed, as O'Shaughnessy says it is. During the course of the tongue's movements it does not loll out of the mouth altogether; presumably this is due to the fact that there is some reason for the tongue not to loll.

O'Shaughnessy suggests another example in passing that would be a problem for the Teleological Theory of Action. 'To be sure, acts can be intentional and done for no reasons, as when one drums one's fingers on the table out of sheer boredom' (1980: ii. 62). This seems more clearly to be a case of intentional action (or at any rate, action), since it seems to be something one makes happen. Then, if the activity is not explainable by a practical justification, this is a counter-example to the Teleological Theory of Action.

But there is no danger of that. For a start, the drumming of one's fingers on the table may be thought to have a practical justification after all. Perhaps the drumming is a way of occupying oneself or of gaining attention, or perhaps one can practically justify such activity in terms of its being an expression of an emotion—in this case, boredom or irritation. Indeed, one might argue that even if the drumming was done for no *further* reason, but was just done for the hell of it, it could still count as practically justified. It would figure right at the top level of a method of practical justification—like an axiom.[2]

The crucial distinction of this chapter can now be made. It is the distinction between two different kinds of teleological explanation of action—externalist explanation and internalist explanation. Put very simply, an externalist explanation does not cite facts about mental states, but only objective facts; whereas an internalist explanation cites only facts about mental states. So, in the case of the asthmatic student, the relevant externalist explanation would be the following:

> I missed assembly because it would have exacerbated my asthma.

A relevant internalist explanation would be:

> I missed assembly because I believed that it would exacerbate my asthma, and I did not want that.

It is important to see that I am using the word 'externalist' in a stronger sense than is usual. One might count an account of the explanation of action to be externalist in a much weaker sense just if the reasons for action were such that one could not have them and at the same time be a brain in a vat. In this sense the reasons might be mental states but they would count as externalist because they presupposed the existence of an external world. In a slightly less weak sense one might think that reasons for action were externalist because one could not have them without the world being just the way represented by those reasons. The reasons might then be mental states but would count as externalist because they were factive—like the states of knowing things or perceiving things. The externalism that I am considering is one according to which the reasons for action do not merely presuppose that there are facts about an external world nor merely presuppose particular facts about the external world but actually *are* themselves facts about the world. 'Internalism' as I am using the term encompasses the two weaker senses of externalism.

---

[2] For a useful treatment of such cases, see Mele (1992: ch. 6).

Suppose that we take the line that every action has an internalist teleological explanation in terms of beliefs, desires, etc. Combining this with the Teleological Theory of Action gives us the conclusion that activity constitutes an action in virtue of being internalistically teleologically explainable. It is because the second student's missing of assembly is appropriately explainable in terms of her beliefs and desires that it constitutes an intentional action. (I am assuming now that she is telling the truth.) The first student's beliefs and desires do not enter into the story of his missing of assembly, and so his missing of assembly is not his action.

Combining the claim that teleological explanation is simply causal explanation in terms of the appropriate beliefs and desires with the Teleological Theory of Action gives us the standard Causal Theory of Action.

> The Causal Theory of Action: Activity resulting in some goal constitutes intentional action directed to that goal in virtue of the activity being caused in an appropriate way by appropriate mental states concerning the goal.

Attention in this area has often been focused on the causal part of this theory. Opponents of the Causal Theory, like Melden (1961), G. H. von Wright (1971), and Stoutland (1982) argue that logical connections between intentions and actions mean that intentions cannot be causes of actions. But concentrating on this argument against the Causal Theory distracts attention from the more interesting aspect of the opposition. Consider this quotation from Melden:

It is impossible to grasp the concepts of motive and desire independently of an action. And, further, the sense in which a motive or a desire explains an item of conduct is altogether different from the sense in which, say, the presence of a spark explains the explosion of a mixture of petrol vapour and air. (Melden 1961: 171–2)

The second sentence of this quotation may well be defended, but not easily if this 'altogether different' sense is taken to be a non-causal sense of explanation. But it is the first sentence that I am interested in. It raises the question of how we attribute intentions and desires to people. We need to know how to attribute these mental states if the Causal Theory is to have any analytical usefulness. Melden's suggestion is that it is only by being able to attribute intentional actions to someone that we can attribute intentions to them.

Certainly there is some constitutive relation going from action to intention. The attribution of an intention based on self-conscious report could be defeated by the evidence that there was no tendency for the subject to act on it. But this does not contradict the Causal Theory. It just means that the Causal Theorist must be satisfied with a holistic account, where there is mutual dependency between attributions of intention and attributions of intentional action.

Suppose, on the other hand, that externalist explanations of action are possible. In this case, we might have a non-holistic account of action and intention after all. Suppose that it is possible to have a complete teleological explanation of action which makes no reference to mental states, but only makes reference to objective facts. Suppose also that the correctness of this externalist explanation is not in virtue of the correctness of some internalist explanation. Combining this with the Teleological Theory of Action gives the conclusion that activity constitutes intentional action in virtue of being explainable by an externalist justification. This means that we could determine whether some activity was an intentional action without reference to the putative agent's mental states.

We can ascribe intentions on the basis of an ascription of intentional action. For, if an intentional action of achieving G has occurred (or would occur in the right circumstances), we can say that the intention to achieve G was present. So an account of externalist teleological explanation would then work as the basis for an account of intentions and also for other mental states. This account would in a sense be behaviourist—I shall call it Teleological Behaviourism. It would say that someone had certain mental states in virtue of their behaviour being teleologically explainable in certain ways.

The assumption that opens the way for Teleological Behaviourism is that externalist explanations of action are possible. However, it is often supposed that there is something inadequate about externalist explanations of action, and that the real, complete, teleological explanations of action must cite internalist reasons after all. This is an example of a philosphical move which I will call the Internalist Shift. Where we might quite naturally think to explain our actions in terms of the facts around us, we are encouraged by the Internalist Shift to look for the true explanation in our own mental states.

Those philosophers who deny the Internalist Shift have tended to link this denial with some claim that weakens the importance of teleological explanation. Some, like Stoutland (1985) and Charlton (1991), deny the causal nature of teleological explanation. Others, like C. Taylor (1964), have denied that teleological explanation is sufficient for intentional action. Taylor, for example, introduces as an extra element the presence of a relevant intention, thus shifting internalistically at a different point in his theory of action. Larry Wright (1976) and Jonathan Bennett (1976) are among the few writers who have tried to construct an account of action purely in terms of externalist explanation.

The rest of this chapter is aimed at undermining the Internalist Shift, while maintaining both the causal nature of teleological explanation and the Teleological Theory of Action. The rest of the book will aim to construct a self-sufficient account of externalist teleological explanation and derive Teleological Behaviourism from it.

There are two ways of questioning the adequacy of purely externalist explanations of action. The first way asks how is it possible for external facts by themselves to rationally *justify* action. The second way asks how is it possible for external facts to be the immediate *causal* reasons for action, since internalist reasons are more immediate. I address these questions in the next two sections.

B. EXTERNALIST JUSTIFICATION OF ACTION

Suppose that you step on my toes and I retaliate by stepping on yours. Assume that in some (not necessarily moral) sense I am justified in doing this. Is it your stepping on my toes that justifies my stepping on yours, or is it only my believing that you stepped on my toes that justifies my action? On the face of it, your stepping on my toes does justify my stepping on your toes quite independently of whether or not I believe you did it. Of course, if I did not believe that you stepped on my toes and I stepped on yours anyway, then in some sense my action would be unjustified. But what this might mean is that I would not be *acting* from a justification. The justification would not explain my action. If we can make sense of the idea of a justification holding good independently of its being currently engaged in action, then it is natural to think of your stepping on my toes as being a justification for my stepping on your toes, but the justification remaining *idle* if I do not believe that you stepped on my toes. I may not be acting for a good reason; but that does not mean that there is no good reason for me to act on.

A deeper motive for denying externalist justification of action is the thought that *desires* must figure in the justification of action. According to this thought, unless I *want* to even the score somehow, then your stepping on my toes provides no justification for my stepping on your toes. This is argued for by Hume at the end of 3.1.1 of his *Treatise*, where he claims that an *ought* can never be derived from an *is*. Motivations cannot be justified through motivationally inert reasoning from motivationally inert facts.

Why not? It seems that *beliefs* can be justified by facts; the fact that you stepped on my toes is the best possible justification for believing that you stepped on my toes. Why should desires and actions not be justified by facts in the same sort of way?

One response to this question might be to point out that a central distinction between beliefs and desires is the direction of fit they have with the world. Successful belief occurs when mental states adapt to the way the world is. However, successful desire and action occur when the way the world is adapts to mental states. What constitutes a justification for the theoretical and the practical cases must reflect this distinction.

But this response simply begs the question at issue. What is at issue is precisely the assumption that successful desire and action only occur when the way the world is adapts to mental states. The externalist alternative is that success in desire and action might be at least partially constituted by the desire and action adapting successfully to the way the world is. This would be to forgo the neat distinction between belief and desire offered by direction of fit. But this should not be a cause for concern; there are other ways of making the distinction.

Another way of defending Hume's claim is to deny that there are the appropriate facts to justify desire and action. There is a fact that you stepped on my toes which can be used to justify directly the belief that you stepped on my toes. But the Humean might argue that it is not a fact that I *should* step on your toes; the world does not contain that sort of fact. In that case, the desire to step on your toes cannot be justified directly by the fact that stepping on your toes is desirable.

But whether or not the world does contain that sort of fact is not really the question at issue here. The fact that P provides some sort of ultimate or direct justification for believing that P. But it is possible to have *false* beliefs which are also justified, but not in this direct way. In such cases the belief that P is not justified by the fact that P; but it does not follow that it is not justified by other facts. It is important to realize that the rational explanation of beliefs and actions that I am considering must extend to cases where the beliefs and actions are not *directly* justified. Actions which are not directly justified can still be teleologically explained using less direct justifications.

We need a relativistic notion of justification to account for beliefs which are not directly justified but which are justified in some indirect way. Such a relativistic notion corresponds with the way we use the word 'should'. It is quite consistent to say that on the one hand I should go to war, while on the other hand I should not go to war. The sentence 'I should go to war and I should not go to war,' is not necessarily a contradiction, for each conjunct may be relative to a different method of justification. Whereas, 'I should go to war and not go to war,' is a clear contradiction, because there is only one 'should' and no room for equivocation about what it is relative to.

A useful way to approach a notion of relativistic justification is by introducing the concept of a *method of deriving a description* of the world. Let the application of such a method issue assents or denials to propositions. There are other ways that the output of such a method might be structured, but this is the simplest. Then we might say that a proposition is justified according to such a method if application of the method yields assent to that proposition. (We might also say that a proposition is *allowed* according to a method, if application of the method does not yield a denial of it.)

A method of deductive inference would count as one such method of deriving a description. But then so would a method of inductive inference. So apparently would a method that resulted in assent to all and only propositions in the Bible. As another example, consider one of the astrological methods of describing people's characters. The method might go as follows. You find out someone's date of birth, look up that date in your copy of 'The Star

Guide to Personality', and assent to any character description you find there. According to this method, I am justified in describing myself as having a fiery temper and being prone to disastrous love affairs, etc. It would be possible for me to believe these things, and for the reason for my believing them to be that I was born on such-and-such a day. My reason might not be a good one; but it is some sort of reason nevertheless.[3]

However, assenting to every single proposition would not count as a method of deriving a description, because it would yield assent to directly contradictory propositions. Any method of deriving a representation of the world (whether linguistic or mental) will automatically be constrained by the fact that a representation cannot embody a direct contradiction. In the same way, perhaps some degree of completeness is also essential to a representation. There are certain sorts of gaps that are not allowed to exist in a description. For example, if '*A* and *B*' is part of a representation, '*A*' must also be part of it. So the products of a method of description are automatically constrained by some minimal degree of coherence.

The psychoanalysis game recently described by Dennett (1991) is a method of deriving conclusions, but not a method of deriving a description. Here you pretend to be describing a dream you had by answering yes or no to another person's questions; but what you are really doing is saying yes if the last letter of the question occurs in the first half of the alphabet, and no otherwise. Applying this method may yield contradictory utterances; so it does not yield a description. Indeed the interest of the game is that the victim assumes that you are applying a method of forming a coherent description, whereas in fact you are only applying a method of forming single conclusions. Utterances may be justified in terms of the method, but judgements may not be. So, your reason for saying 'No, I was not dreaming about a white unicorn,' is that the last letter of the question comes in the second half of the alphabet. But a judgement cannot be justified in such a way. For the same method simultaneously gives reason for accepting other utterances of the same proposition: e.g. 'Were you dreaming of a unicorn that was white?'

The question of this section can now be put in the following terms. Are there any further constraints on which methods of

---

[3] Compare this with Dennett's discussion of the astrological strategy (1987: 16).

deriving descriptions should count as methods of *justification*; and if so do they rule out purely externalist justification of action? I will only consider (and reject) one suggestion for such a constraint now. In Chapter 4 I will look at the notion of practical justification more closely.

It might be thought that no method can count as properly justifying something unless one can find some reason for accepting the method. The method of justification must itself be justified. Let me describe this as the demand that justifications be *total*. This demand for the totality of a justification seems to require that justifications involve never-ending systems of nested justifications. If a method of justification must itself be justified by another method of justification, then the other method of justification will need to be justified, and so on. However, the infinite regress will be stopped if a method of justification may be justified in some more basic way that does not depend on another method of justification.

We see this sort of consideration at work in the traditional debate about induction. The search is for some basic way of justifying the inductive method which does not itself need justifying. One such way would be to show that the method has deductive validity. This was Hume's main target in his treatment of induction. Another is the move of saying that it is part of what we mean by justification that the inductive method works. More modern theories of knowledge urge that all that is required is that the inductive method be reliable or that it discriminates truth from falsity.

But whatever the merits of these suggestions, in the context of looking for a total justification, they fall short. The question of further justification can always be raised (e.g. why should we follow a method that is reliable?). And, according to the requirement of total justification, if the question can be raised, part of the justification must be an answer to it.

So the demand for a total justification can never be satisfied. I take this to be a good reason for thinking that the demand is too stringent. But even if it could be satisfied it would be too stringent. For it simply rules out of court the possibility of bad justification. It must be a mistake to stipulate that I cannot believe something for (e.g.) astrological reasons.

In the case of practical justification, the demand for total justification is expressed in the following argument. Suppose you ask someone: 'Why should you do *X*?' Then, after every response they give, you ask: 'Why should that count as a reason?' They will eventually run out of external reasons and be forced to cut the inquisition short with the reply: 'Because I want to.'

But, as with the theoretical case, no such move can ever close the inquisition. It is still available to the inquisitor to ask 'Why does wanting something count as a reason for acting to get it?' One might be a Buddhist who regards wanting something to be a reason for withdrawing oneself from it. The demand for a total justification will demand a justification for being a desire-fulfiller rather than a desire-denier. This will be so even if one thinks that it is part of what it is to want to do something that one will do it if nothing gets in the way. For one would still need to justify not putting anything in the way. I am not saying that there are no good arguments for in general doing what you want to do. What I am saying is that 'because I want to' does not totally close a justification. For there are no totally closed justifications.

I think, however, that the blank rejection of the demand for ultimate or total justification does leave some intuition about the point of justification unsatisfied. Although justifications do not have to be total, isn't it essential to justifications that they be *on the way* to being total? You should aim at the truth with your beliefs and at rightness with your actions; and a method for deriving descriptions which does not belong to a higher-order process of improving methods of justification in line with this aim does not count as a method of *justification* at all.

This intuition is present in Hegel's notion of the dialectical process.[4] For Hegel, thought is essentially a dynamic process. It starts by representing the world as though this representation gives the complete truth. This is the Abstract Stage. But when thought takes itself as its own object, it starts to yield contradictions. This is the Dialectical Stage. It must then unify the contradictory representations in some higher-order mode of representation. This is the Speculative Stage. Then the cycle begins again.

For Hegel, this dialectical process is essential to the nature of thought; I am presenting the intuition that a similar dialectical process is essential to the nature of justification. It is not just a

[4] See Hegel's *Logic*, translated in part in Hegel (1989 edn.: ch. 8).

contingent psychological fact that superior methods of justification supersede inferior ones; but it should follow from the nature of justification.

Post-modernist philosophers, like Lyotard (1984 edn.), argue, as I have been arguing, against the need for total justifications. But part of their argument is against the necessity of the dialectical process. They argue that there is no need to look for higher-order methods of justification to resolve incompatible lower-order ones. So they reject the Hegelian intuition that I am trying to accommodate.

The dialectical process may be represented as involving the following stages:

1. (The Abstract Stage) Work within a single method of justification.
2. (The Dialectical Stage) Learn alternative and incompatible methods of justification.
3. (The Speculative Stage) Work out a higher-order method of justification which supersedes the methods of stage 2 and enables rationally motivated choice to be made between them.
4. Go to stage 1.

Post-modernism recommends not going to stage 3, but stopping at stage 2, playing with methods of practical justification but never developing the resources to become committed to any particular one. If this post-modern condition is indeed our condition (even if we are too dogmatic, as the post-modernists suggest, to see that it is) then perhaps we can derive another sort of argument for including desire in every practical justification.

Consider the analogy with playing games. Part of what it is to know how to play a particular game (e.g. patience) is to know that it is optional whether or not one plays. The rules of the game seem to admit the possibility of not playing the game. One is not going against the rules of a game by not embarking on the game at all.

This would be paradoxical were it not the case that the rules of a game are embedded in a larger structure which says what you should do *if* you play patience, but is quite indeterminate as to whether you should or shouldn't play patience. This larger structure issues hypothetical imperatives. So, in order for the method to yield any description of a move in patience rather than a move in some other game, it must take into account the current preferences of the agent. The fact that you *want* to play patience must figure in your justification of playing a move in patience.

The situation is that we have a lot of different sets of rules that we might follow even with a simple pack of cards. But we have no set of rules telling us which of these sets of rules to adopt at any one time. So, our total set of rules does not tell us what we should do at any one moment. We need something like a desire to fill in this indeterminacy in our overall justification.

The same sort of analysis is applied by post-modernists beyond the realm of games. Given that we learn a number of incompatible methods of justification, and assuming that there is no higher-order method available, how could it be otherwise than that we work from an overall system that is indifferent as to which is chosen. The only thing that can justify the use of one method of justification rather than another is blank preference.

The condition of being faced with a choice and having no reason to go one way rather than the other is described by existentialists as Anguish. There is a very useful example of this given by Sartre (1973 edn.) and discussed by C. Taylor (1977) of a boy in Occupied France who is torn between staying at home to look after his dying mother and going away to fight for the liberation of his country. The boy is faced with two incompatible ways of life and has got no method of justification available that will enable him to choose between them.

Apparently, however, the post-modernists (as exemplified, perhaps unfairly, by Lyotard) feel no anxiety about this condition. This may be because, despite what they say, they have articulated a higher-order method of justification after all. This would be the method according to which it is better not to undercut one method of justification from the standpoint of another, but always to do it from within, through a process of deconstruction. It is better to flirt with methods according to the way you feel, but never to get committed to one. If post-modernists are really following this higher-order method, it would mean that they do not really occupy the space between stages 2 and 3 after all; but are resolutely stuck at stage 1.

Indeed it is difficult to see how it is even possible to occupy the position that post-modernists claim to occupy. If you had no reason to choose one method rather than another, it seems wrong to say that *you* were engaged in the choice at all. Of course, if you choose to go whichever way blank preference takes you, then you are involved in the choice. This is why choosing a *mille-feuille* rather than a chocolate éclair does count as your choice even when all you consult is what you feel like doing. You are working with a method according to which you should at such times do what you feel like doing. This is where desires are incorporated into your method of justification, but not at the very bottom level. It is not the bottom level because of the further decision to do what you feel like doing. But the position I am considering to be the post-modernist position is one where there is no higher-order consideration operating. There are no resources here with which to deny that you are drawn quite passively one way or the other by your preferences. In this sort of situation, if you want to be justified in your choice, you must get some control and work out a motivation for preferring one method rather than another.[5]

So, I think that there are two possible things that might happen to the boy in Sartre's example. The first is that he might end his Anguish by working out some higher-order method of justification which decides the issue. This method will not itself be justified for the time being. Whatever psychological forces make him work out that particular method will not themselves be incorporated in any justification, for, by hypothesis, the method he has just worked out is the highest-order method. Of course, this method will itself be vulnerable to a continuation of the dialectical process; but it will be a temporary place to locate himself.

The higher-order method of justification will issue categorical, not hypothetical, imperatives. These imperatives are relative to the method of justification, but are not conditional on it. This is because, at this stage, he has not got the luxury of occupying a perspective outside his highest-order method (see McDowell 1978). So, instead of having rationally unmotivated preferences at the bottom level, he has rationally unmotivated methods of justification.

The second possibility for the boy in Sartre's example is that he fails to cure his Anguish. If the boy is going to keep suffering from Anguish, it will not do him any good at all to say that he simply prefers the option of adopting the freedom-fighting way of life. This

---

[5] This is argued for in C. Taylor (1977).

is because he will worry about why he should do what he prefers to do. The fact that he is eventually drawn one way rather than the other will not itself be justified. Whatever psychological forces and inclinations cause him to go one way or the other are not part of his justification. We have now gone beyond justification into pure psychology.[6] Indeed it seems quite wrong to call these basic psychological forces and inclinations 'desires' at all. It is only when we can be self-conscious about such forces and incorporate them into our methods of justification that we call them wants and desires. The forces that determine what our ultimate method of justification is are themselves necessarily outside justification. So at the bottom level of a justification we do not find the agent's intentions and desires; nor do we find a more primitive set of psychological forces. What we find is the method of justification itself.

C. THE IMMEDIATE CAUSES OF ACTION

The second apparent difficulty with the proposal that actions may have a purely externalist explanation is the thought that internal reasons, e.g. beliefs, always have a more immediate *causal* role in explaining action. Facts alone cannot comprise the most immediate, basic, causal explanation of action; for action is not directly sensitive to facts, but only to mental states representing (or misrepresenting) the facts.

There are two sides to this argument. The first side I shall call the Argument from False Beliefs. The possibility that false beliefs (i.e. beliefs which do not have corresponding facts) motivate actions just as well as true ones do is supposed to show that it does not make any difference to the fundamental explanation of action whether the agent's beliefs are true or false. I shall call the other side of the argument the Argument from the Impotence of Unrepresented Facts. It begins with the observation that a fact, however true, cannot motivate action unless it is believed (or known). So it must be the mental state of belief (or knowledge) which is doing the causal work, and not the fact.

[6] Of course, once the boy has for whatever reason been drawn to one way of justifying himself rather than the other, then his Anguish may disappear. This would be because from within one of the two ways of life, the other one is not available. He would have burnt his boats.

The Argument from False Beliefs claims to point out that it does not matter as far as the causal explanation of action is concerned whether the relevant belief does or does not have a corresponding fact. The Argument from the Impotence of Unrepresented Facts claims to point out that it *does* matter crucially to the causal explanation of action whether or not the relevant fact has a corresponding belief. Together, they seem to show that it is to the beliefs and not to the corresponding facts that action is directly causally sensitive. I want to deny this apparently obvious set of claims.

I shall begin by spelling out the Argument from False Beliefs. When an agent acts on false beliefs, we cannot explain the action in terms of the facts but only in terms of those beliefs—there is only an internalist explanation of their action. But even when the beliefs are true that same internalist explanation works. The differences between cases where the beliefs are true and cases where they are not are all in the world outside the agent. In terms of the immediate explanation of the agent's behaviour there is no difference between the cases. So the same internalist explanation must lie at the core of all explanations of action whether the beliefs are true or false.

According to this story, action can still be explained in terms of facts, but only in terms of a two-part account. The first part is the explanation of the formation of beliefs in terms of the facts. The second part is the explanation of action in terms of belief. Epistemology should deal with the first, and the Philosophy of Action should deal only with the second.

The Argument from False Beliefs is captured precisely in the following form:

P1. When an agent acts on the basis of false beliefs, the causal reasons for their action are beliefs and not external facts.
P2. The rational (causal) explanation of the agent's action in terms of false beliefs works just as well when those beliefs are true.

Therefore:

C. External facts do not figure in the most immediate rational explanations of action, even in the case of acting on true beliefs.

At the heart of this argument is the concept of the most immediate level of explanation. This needs some elucidation. I may explain the death of a tree in terms of an unusually mild winter, but the more immediate reason is the honey fungus infestation which the mild winter allowed. And presumably there will be still more immediate explanations (the strangulation of the xylem channels by the fungus, the loss of nutrients in the cells, etc.).

So, one explanation of a phenomenon is less immediate than another if the first explanation can be spelled out in a way so that the second explanation is a proper part of it. The more immediate explanation in this sense is thereby analytically more basic. For the less immediate explanation holds only in virtue of the more immediate explanation holding. If internalist explanations of action are explanatorily more immediate than externalist explanations of action, it follows that we should account for the teleological explanation of action in terms of internalist explanations. Externalist explanations would have only a secondary role.

The argument as it stands is not valid. Some assumption like the following needs to be added to it.

> P3. If phenomenon *P* can be completely explained without reference to *X*, then *X* is not an essential part of an immediate explanation of *P*.

According to P3, there can never be two distinct but equally immediate explanations of the same thing. This means that we would have to make a choice between an internalist and an externalist explanation of action in terms of explanatory immediacy. In which case, it seems clear that we would have to choose the internalist explanation.

Given this, we can see that the Argument from False Beliefs only works if rational explanations of the same action are taken to fit into a single scale in which internalist explanations are either more or less immediate than externalist explanations. The sort of picture that leads to this assumption is one in which the explanation of action belongs to a series of Russian dolls with the explanandum in the centre. We can strip off the outer layers of explanation by changing the facts so that the beliefs are false. But, if the internalist layer remains, it will still explain the action. Because of the possibility of false beliefs in which the internalist explanation works and the externalist explanation fails, the internalist explanation must occupy a more central place in the nest of explanations than the externalist explanation.

In fact, the conclusion of the Argument from False Beliefs is even stronger that I have suggested. Not only must facts be excluded from the most immediate explanation of action, but so must fact-involving mental states, like perceiving, knowing, etc. According to the argument, the explanation of an action in terms of seeing that it satisfies some goal is less immediate than the explanation of it in terms of *believing* that it satisfies the goal. So only *strongly* internalist mental states (i.e. those whose identity is independent of the truth or existence of what they are about) should figure in a basic explanation of action. The Argument from False Beliefs cannot be used for denying the propriety of purely externalist explanations of action without at the same time forcing on one a fairly radical internalism about the explanation of action.

It should also be noted that the Argument from False Beliefs exactly mirrors one of the most dangerous arguments in epistemology—namely, the causal version of the Argument from Illusion. The conclusion of the Argument from Illusion is that only strongly internal states, like appearances, should figure in the immediate rational (causal) explanation of perceptual beliefs.

The parallels between epistemology and the philosophy of action are very marked. Whereas in the explanation of action, the reason *practically* justifies the action, in the explanation of belief, the reason *theoretically* justifies the belief. But in each case, the object is being explained in terms of a justification of it. As with the explanation of action, in the explanation of belief both externalist and internalist explanations are possible.

An example of an externalist epistemological explanation is the following:

> I believe that there is a fly in the room because a fly just came in at the open window.

An internalist equivalent is:

> I believe that there is a fly in the room because it appears to me as if a fly just came in at the open window.

And another internalist explanation which is not strongly internalist but cites fact-involving mental states is:

> I believe that there is a fly in the room because I saw one come in at the open window.

Given this, we can frame an epistemological Internalist Shift parallel to the Internalist Shift for action. According to this, externalist explanations of belief can only hold good in virtue of more immediate internalist explanations holding good. And one of the arguments that leads one to this conclusion is the following version of the Argument from Illusion.

P1*. When a subject forms a perceptual belief on the basis of illusion, the causal reasons for the belief are appearances and not external facts.

P2*. The explanation of the subject's belief in terms of appearances works just as well when the subject forms that belief on the basis of veridical experience as it does when the subject is undergoing an illusion.

P3. If phenomenon P can be completely explained without reference to X, then X is not an essential part of any immediate explanation of P.

Therefore:

C*. External facts do not figure in the most immediate explanations of perceptual belief, even in the case of veridical experience.

This conclusion has been perceived by many philosophers as being at the root of unanswerable sceptical arguments. And a number of ways have been sought to deny it. Proponents of the disjunctive approach to appearances deny P2* (see Hinton 1973; Snowdon 1981, 1990; and McDowell 1982).

But suppose we say—not at all unnaturally—that an appearance that such-and-such is the case can be either a mere appearance or the fact that such-and-such is the case making itself perceptually manifest to someone. As before, the object of experience in the deceptive cases is a mere appearance. But we are not to accept that in the non-deceptive cases too the object of experience is a mere appearance, and hence something that falls short of the fact itself. On the contrary, we are to insist that the appearance that is presented to one in those cases is a matter of the fact itself being disclosed to the experiencer. So appearances are no longer conceived as in general intervening between the experiencing subject and the world. (McDowell 1982: 472)

According to this account, the internal state that explains an illusory perceptual belief just is not present in veridical perception. So the explanation of the illusory belief does not carry over to the explanation in the veridical case.

I think that denying P2* is the wrong way to attack the Argument from Illusion. In convincing illusion, a subject is not aware of the illusoriness of the experience; so they are not aware of the *mereness* of the appearance. To take the object of experience to go beyond what the subject is aware of is to compromise the essential subjectivity of experience.

An alternative way of countering the Argument from Illusion is to deny P3. This is to deny that explanations of the same thing must fit into a single scale in which the less immediate explanations contain the more immediate explanations. This way has the advantage of countering the Argument from False Beliefs at the same time. In the next chapter I develop a pluralistic account of causal explanation that will support this denial. What will emerge is that internalist and externalist explanations belong to quite different categories of explanation and so cannot be placed in a single scale, one more immediate than the other. P3 will be shown to be false, and neither the Argument from False Beliefs nor the causal version of the Argument from Illusion (as I have stated them) will work.

It is very important to have found a way of denying the Argument from False Beliefs. For, if we were forced to accept it, then we would have to accept not only strong internalism about the reasons for action, but also internalism about action itself. We would, in fact, have to accept that actions did not extend into the world. The argument is as follows.

Assume that the Argument from False Beliefs is correct, and therefore that the teleological explanation of an action need only work with strongly internalist reasons like beliefs and desires. (Recall that what I mean by a strongly internalist state is one whose existence is independent of whether or not it corresponds with anything in the world.) Such an explanation will explain the action *via* explanation of the internal effort to do that action. A strongly internalist explanation of an action describes a process that begins with states like beliefs and desires and ends with an action. Somewhere along the way the process must break through from a domain involving only strongly internal states to one involving external states. Call the last stage before this breakthrough the internal effort. The internal effort might be thought of as the process of actively intending to do the action until it is apparently achieved. It is supposed to represent the purely internal part of what goes on in an action.

But if the action had external parts which the internal effort did not have, then the move from the internal effort to the action itself would not be explained in terms of strongly internalist practical reasons. It would depend on external considerations that are independent of the practical reasons. So, what is teleologically explainable is only that part of the process which concerns the internal effort. In the process, there is no sensitivity to strongly internalist practical reasons beyond that; so the teleological process cannot break through to the external parts of the action.

The Teleological Theory of Action says that activity constitutes intentional action in virtue of being explainable in terms of a practical justification. We have seen that the external part of the process is not explainable in terms of strongly internalist practical justification. Given this, the only activity that genuinely constitutes the action is the internal effort. So, assuming the Teleological Theory of Action and strong internalism about the teleological explanation of action, it follows that actions are no more than internal efforts.

It should be stressed that this internalism about actions does not follow from internalism about teleological explanation of action, but only from *strong* internalism about teleological explanation of action. If world-involving mental states, like knowing, perceiving, etc., had to be included in the most immediate explanation of action, then there would be no reason to suppose that world-involving actions cannot be explained by them. So, internalism about action does not follow directly from the Internalist Shift in the explanation of action, but only from one argument for the Internalist Shift, namely the Argument from False Beliefs, according to which even world-involving mental states should not be included in the most immediate explanation of action.

On the face of it, this consequence of accepting the Argument from False Beliefs is disastrously sceptical. Our strongest intuition is that action involves interaction with objects, not just an interplay of mental events. However Hornsby, in her book *Actions* (Hornsby 1980), feels able to accept this sceptical consequence. She does this by extending Davidson's strategy of distinguishing between the identity of an event and descriptions of that event. We may describe

events (actions in particular) in terms of things which have nothing
to do with the identity of those events.

Consider Davidson's example (travestying Hamlet) of the queen
killing the king by pouring poison in his ear (1980: 55). The death
of the king is essential if the event is to be described as a killing. But,
according to Davidson (and Hornsby), the death is not part of the
event at all; the very same event could occur without it being
describable as a killing. For after the queen's hand has moved to tip
the poison she 'has done her work; it only remains for the poison to
do its' (Davidson 1980: 58). The event which is the action of killing
the king is over before the king has died.

According to Hornsby's extension of this strategy, even the moving of the queen's hand is not genuinely part of the event which is
her killing the king. Hornsby claims that once the queen has *tried*
to move her hand, the action is done; there is nothing more for her
to do. Apparently, the actual movement of her hand is no part of
the event which is her trying to move her hand.

This position is not obviously counter-intuitive. Most of the
things we want to say about actions we can still say. When we talk
of actions involving external objects, this could be understood as
providing descriptions of an internal event in terms of its effects on
external objects. And where this theory does run counter to intuition, the intuitions do not clearly decide the issue. For example,
according to Hornsby (citing an experiment by William James),
when a blindfolded anaesthetized person who is trying to raise her
arm at the same time as it is being held down, becomes convinced
that she is successful, exactly the same event occurs as occurs when
her arm is not held down and she does raise it. Although it may
seem odd to say this, Hornsby has no difficulty in accepting it. So,
the matter cannot be settled against Hornsby simply by examining
the intuitions in such cases.

Actions are naturally thought of as causal *processes*. This is
argued for by Dretske (1988: 16 ff.). He takes this to prove that
actions cannot be entirely internal, but must include their intended
effects. Certainly, it seems right to say that the process of the queen
killing the king can extend through time and space beyond the
internal effort and the body movement to the ultimate death of the
king. This seems right in the same way that it seems right to say that
the causal process of the sun melting a piece of butter extends
beyond the sun's production of heat to the butter's melting.

But Dretske's inference from this to the conclusion that actions are external is too quick. It does not follow from the fact that actions are causal processes that that very causal process of the queen killing the king that includes the king's death is an action. For there are several processes going on here, not all of which are actions. We might accept that there is an action which is the causal process of the queen *intentionally* killing the king, but refuse to identify this with that process of the queen killing the king which includes the king dying. Whereas it seems intuitively right to talk of that process of the queen killing the king continuing after the queen has gone back to sleep, it is far less natural to talk of the action which is the process of the queen intentionally killing the king continuing while she is asleep in bed. What is going on in the king seems to have too little to do with her to count as part of the process of her intentionally acting.

What is lacking from Davidson, Hornsby, and Dretske is some acceptable principle for deciding which process or part of the process of the queen killing the king is sufficiently tied up with her agency to count as the process of her acting intentionally to kill the king. We have three different answers to the question of what constitutes the causal process that is the intentional action— namely: the body movement, the internal effort, the causal process ending in the intended effect—but we have no principled way of choosing between them.

One principle that seems quite promising here is that proposed by Adam Morton (1975: 14).

Intentional action is action that is guided by information to which it is responsive.

This captures a position between that of Davidson and that of Dretske. After the queen has poured the poison, her behaviour is not responsive to whether the poison ends up working or not. (We assume that she goes straight back to sleep after pouring the poison.) So, if we accept Morton's principle and identify the intentional action with the process of guided response, the intentional action is not going on after the queen goes back to sleep. All that her behaviour responds to is information concerning what is required to *make a good shot* at killing the king. What happens after that is not part of the process.

But, if the queen waited up over the king after pouring the

poison, ready to stab him to death if the poison failed to work, then the process of guided response would extend much further. Even if she did not have to do anything but wait for him to die, it no longer feels at all convincing to say that her action is over once her hand has moved and the poison has been poured. Waiting to see whether the poison works in readiness to inflict some further blow if it does not is part of the process of intentionally *making sure that the king dies*.

If the agent is only responsive to whether or not she is making a good shot at killing the king, then making the good shot at it is all that is properly part of the action; and she is not still acting after she has made that shot at it. If her behaviour is responsive to whether he dies, then his dying is part of her action; and she is still acting after she has poured the poison, even though her body may be relatively still.

Morton's principle leads to a position that is clearly distinct from both Davidson's and Dretske's. It is not immediately obvious that it is contradicted by Hornsby's, however. For the process of guided response lasts exactly as long as the internal effort lasts. In the first case, the queen's effort stops after the poison has been poured, whereas, in the second case, she is trying to kill the king right up until the moment he dies. So, Hornsby and Morton can agree on the temporal dimensions of action.

Also, it might be thought that Morton's principle does not commit us to spatial externalism about action. It might be said that a process of guided response is a process of producing *internal efforts* in response to how things *seem* to be going with one's goals—i.e. a completely internal process. However, this thought is rather artificial. There is no good reason in general to limit a process of guided response to being an internal process. If external behaviour can be responsive to what is required for some external goal to be achieved, then we can have external processes of guided response, and hence external actions.

This is not conclusive. A lot of the groundwork necessary for an externalist account of action will be done in later chapters. But, if there is any plausibility at this stage to the view that actions are at least partly external, then we have good reason to look for a way to deny strong internalism about teleological explanation. In order to do this, we must deny the Argument from False Beliefs.

It is now time to consider the other argument in favour of

the Internalist Shift that was mentioned at the beginning of the section—namely the Argument from the Impotence of Unrepresented Facts. This, roughly, is the argument that if a fact is not mentally represented by the agent, then it cannot figure in the explanation of her action; so it cannot be the fact as such, but rather the mental state representing the fact that is the immediate reason for action.

Unlike the Argument from False Beliefs this does not result in *strong* internalism about reasons for action, but only in weak internalism. It requires that mental states must figure in the most immediate explanation of action, but does not require that those mental states be capable of existing independently of the truth of what they represent.

One version of this argument is Hume's in the *Treatise*, 2.3.3. He claims that 'reason alone can never be a motive to any action of the will' (Hume 1888 edn.: 413). This is designed to show that an agent's motivating reasons for an action must include desires (or other passions) as well as beliefs. (The Internalist Shift as far as beliefs are concerned is already embedded in Hume's empiricist theory of ideas.)

The basis of Hume's argument is that practical reasoning alone cannot take one from a state without a motivational element (a passion) to a state with such a motivational element. Reason alone cannot inject passion; it can only redirect passion to its proper object.

The simplest way to fill in the argument for Hume's conclusion is to make the following observation: *unless an agent had some appropriate desire they would have no reason to act.* This observation is clearly true. It may be thought to follow equally clearly from this that the desire must be one of the agent's reasons to act. But it does not follow, as McDowell, taking his argument from T. Nagel (1970: 29–30), shows:

> the commitment to ascribe such a desire is simply consequential on our taking him to act as he does for the reason we cite; the desire does not function as an extra component in a full specification of his reason. (McDowell 1978: 15)

The fact that there is a conceptual connection between having a desire and having a reason for one's action need not be explained by the fact that one has a reason for one's action in virtue of having the desire. It may be explained by the fact that one has the desire in virtue of having a reason for one's action; that is in virtue of the reason explaining or potentially explaining one's action.

The point here is that there may be a behaviourist account of desire, or, at least, of some desires. According to such an account, what it is to want to do something—say to poison one's husband— is not to be thought of as a causally isolatable entity in the mind. Instead, it is to be thought of as having the goal of poisoning one's husband as what actually and potentially motivates one's actions. If it is possible to explain externalistically the queen's pouring some liquid into her husband's ear just in terms of the fact that that is a way to poison her husband, then that will justify our attributing to her the desire to poison her husband. There might be no conscious recognition of this desire; it simply consists in the disposition to act to achieve that goal.

This account, in which desire has no primary role in the explana- tion of action, but is ascribed to an agent merely in *consequence* of some more immediate explanation, derives from Kant's dis- cussion of 'reverence' in the *Groundwork of the Metaphysics of Morals*.

Yet although reverence is a feeling, it is not a feeling *received* through outside influence, but one *self-produced* by a rational concept, and there- fore specifically distinct from feelings of the first kind, all of which can be reduced to inclination or fear. What I recognize immediately as law for me, I recognize with reverence, which means merely consciousness of the *subordination* of my will to a law without the mediation of external influences on my senses. Immediate determination of the will by the law and consciousness of this determination is called '*reverence*', so that rever- ence is regarded as the *effect* of the law on the subject and not as the *cause* of the law. (Kant 1948 edn.: 66–7 n.)

This Kantian strategy for accounting for the role of desires in the explanation of action may be extended to account for the role of beliefs. For (to rephrase the earlier McDowell quotation) the com- mitment to ascribe a belief may be simply consequential on our taking the agent to act as they do, for the reason we cite; the belief need not function as an independent extra component in a full specification. According to this behaviourist line, beliefs should be attributed in virtue of an agent's activity or potential activity being explained (or potentially explained) by the relevant external facts according to a method of justification that works as if the beliefs were true.[7]

Williams, in his paper 'Internal and External Reasons' (1981: 106–7), gives the following argument for including beliefs in any full explanation of action:

> Now no external reason statement could *by itself* offer an explanation of anyone's action. Even if it were true (whatever that might turn out to mean) that there was a reason for Owen to join the army, that fact by itself would never explain anything that Owen did, not even his joining the army. For if it was true at all, it was true when Owen was not motivated to join the army. The whole point of external reason statements is that they can be true independently of the agent's motivations. But nothing can explain an agent's (intentional) actions except something that motivates him so to act. So something else is needed besides the truth of the external reason statement to explain action, some psychological link; and that psychological link would seem to be belief.

If we take this argument at face value, it has the following form:

A. An external fact may or may not motivate an agent.
B. Any reason which explains an action must motivate the agent.
C. So an external fact cannot be a reason which explains an action.

Let us assume that by 'reason' we mean 'motivating reason'. Then, the same external fact may in one situation be a reason and in another situation not be a reason. Which one it is depends on whether the agent's activity is explained by it. So Williams's argument is invalid because there is the possibility that an external fact may or may not motivate an agent; when it does not motivate it is not a reason, but when it does motivate it is a reason.

Perhaps what underlies Williams's argument is a certain theory of explanation in which a complete specification of the reasons must form a logically sufficient condition of the thing being explained. According to this theory, if there is a valid explanation of some result in terms of a complete set of reasons, then it is impossible that in some other situation all those reasons should be true and yet the corresponding result not happen. If a complete explana-

---

[7] The details of such a behaviourist account are given in Chapter 5.

tion needs to include in its reasons something which distinguishes the case of the impotent fact from the case where the fact motivates, it looks as if some internal element will be required.

It would follow from such a theory of explanation that every possible brain malfunction would have to be ruled out in the reasons for action. I suspect it would then be impossible ever to get an explanation going. In the next chapter I aim to provide an alternative theory of explanation. But, even accepting this very strong requirement on explanation, internalism about reasons for action still does not follow. What does follow, as Williams asserts, is that some psychological element is needed in a complete explanation of action. But we need not conclude that this element is a belief. Having to include some psychological element in a complete immediate explanation of action falls very far short of making the Internalist Shift.

I have now countered the most powerful arguments for the position that action cannot be directly causally sensitive to external facts, but only to mental states. But I have yet to produce an argument for the position that action must, at least sometimes, be directly explained only in terms of external facts. This book is largely an attempt to construct an account of the explanation of action in terms of external facts. Here is an argument for the need of such an account.[8]

Assume that strong internalism about action is false. Then, according to my earlier argument, strong internalism about the immediate reasons for action is false also. Assume also (*per impossibile*) that purely externalist immediate explanations of action are not possible, but that some teleological explanation of action *is* possible.

Strong internalism about teleological explanation of action cannot be avoided merely by including some external facts in the explanation alongside the strongly internal mental states. For these facts, which would be represented by the strongly internal mental states, would have to drop out of the immediate explanation as quite redundant. (Or else, the strongly internal mental states would have to drop out as redundant.)

---

[8] Large arguments like the one I am about to offer are dangerous. There are too many ways in which an opponent committed to denying the conclusion might undermine it. But, at least it offers a structure within which such an opponent may define their opposition.

The only way to avoid strong internalism is to include as reasons for action mental states which are not strongly internal. One such state might be that of the subject *being aware that* P. For this state to satisfy its role of keeping in play a position between strong internalism and externalism it must not be reducible to a combination of strongly internalist and purely externalist parts. Otherwise, the externalist part would have to drop out as redundant to the explanation.

For this reason, a standard causal account of awareness, in which awareness of P consists in P causing some strongly internal mental representation of P, is ruled out. But some sort of causal input account of awareness must be right. For, to account for the fact of P itself being an essential part of the state, an account of the state must take us all the way back to P. (I am assuming that there is *some* account possible of awareness.)

We have ruled out an input account of awareness in which P has a causal influence on a *strongly internal state*. This seems to leave only two possible sorts of input account. Either, the subject being aware of P involves P causally explaining the subject's *behaviour*. Or, the subject being aware of P involves P causally explaining some *non-strongly internal state* of the subject.

According to the first possibility, we have externalist explanation of behaviour. Of course, this need not be the most immediate explanation—some internal state may mediate. But, in that case, the external fact would have to drop out of the picture again as redundant, and the account would collapse into strong internalism. The second possibility merely pushes the argument into a further cycle concerning the nature of this new non-strongly internal state. At the end of all the cycles, if we are to avoid strong internalism about teleological explanation of action, we must accept the possibility of purely externalist teleological explanation of action.

D. AWARENESS OF ONE'S REASONS FOR ACTION

One final argument that might be put forward for the Internalist Shift is an epistemological one. It begins with the assumption that one cannot be directly aware of external facts, but only of internal ones, like seemings, believings, desires, etc. A second assumption is that an agent's teleological reasons for action must be things that the agent is directly aware of. It follows immediately from these two assumptions that external facts cannot be among an agent's teleological reasons for action.

I think that the second assumption is correct. If the agent did not have some immediate mental access to the reasons for their behaviour, then the involvement of their agency in this behaviour would be brought into question. The immediate reasons for an agent's action must be *their* reasons.

So my denial of the Internalist Shift does not involve me in denying that an agent must have mental access to the immediate reasons for their actions. Instead, it involves me in denying the first assumption that an agent cannot have mental access to external reasons for action.

This assumption, that an agent cannot have mental access to external reasons, can be derived from the causal version of the Argument from Illusion as described earlier. In this case, it depends on the questionable theory of explanation embodied in P3. But it can also be derived from a more direct version of the Argument from Illusion based on a Cartesian assumption about the nature of direct awareness.

(1) What a subject is directly aware of is given by how things seem to that subject.

Combine this with two relatively innocuous assumptions about hallucination.

(2) In hallucination the subject is not directly aware of a real object or external fact.

(3) For every veridical perception there is a possible hallucination that seems to the subject to be identical to it.

The combination of assumptions (1) and (3) results in the conclusion that in perception the subject is directly aware of exactly the same as they would be in the corresponding hallucination. Combining this with (2), we must conclude that even in perception the subject is not directly aware of any real objects or external facts.

The Cartesian assumption, (1), is doing all the work in this argument. Since the way things seem is independent of whether or not things are actually as they seem, it follows directly from (1) that experience is strongly internal in the sense defined earlier.

Assumption (1) seems at first sight to be nothing more than an articulation of the subjectivity of experience. But it is important to see that it involves a significant additional assumption, namely that how things *are* in the subject's experience is given by how things *seem* to the subject.

This assumption is now taken for granted by many philosophers. It is encapsulated in the slogan that the subjective nature of experience is given by what it is *like* to have that experience.[9] A convincing hallucination is just like the real thing. So what it is *like* to have a hallucination is the same as what it is *like* to perceive the real thing. It would then follow that as far as their subjective natures are concerned the two experiences are the same.

But I think that one needs to examine very carefully what the word 'like' is doing in this slogan. We are interested not in what an experience is *like* but in what an experience *is*. What it means to say that a hallucination is like the real thing is that the hallucination *seems* like the real thing. So the identification of subjective *experience* with *appearance* is smuggled in by this sort of talk. If we are not to beg the question in favour of the Cartesian assumption (1), we must not automatically identify how things are for a subject's experience with what things are like for a subject.

In the course of this book I will lay down the foundations of an alternative account of what it is for a subject to be directly aware of something. It will emerge that a subject is directly aware of something if that thing is present to the subject's teleological processes. It follows from this that if something is a teleological reason for the subject's behaviour, then the subject is *thereby* aware of it.

---

[9] See Nagel's identification of how things are from the subject's point of view with what it is like to be that subject in 'What is it like to be a bat?' (Nagel 1978: 165–80). My argument against identifying how things are for the subject with how they seem to the subject is strongly influenced by McDowell (1982 and elsewhere).

2

Causal Explanation

A. INTRODUCTION

I have three reasons for interpolating a chapter on causal explanation into a book about agency. First, in Chapter 1 I claimed that both the Argument from False Beliefs and the Argument from the Impotence of Unrepresented Facts depend on bad theories of explanation. To make this claim convincing I must show what is wrong with the bad theories and provide a good theory in their place.

Secondly, I want to show that teleological explanation is a species of causal explanation, and I want to show how an account of teleological explanation emerges quite naturally from an account of causal explanation in general. Much of the philosophical literature on teleological explanation seems to be distorted for failing to take this route. When we have in place a good account of what explanation is in general, the necessary and sufficient conditions for teleological explanation, which appear *ad hoc* according to most accounts, can be seen to follow simply from the fact that teleological explanation is explanation in terms of a means-end practical justification.

Thirdly, providing an account of causal explanation gives me an opportunity to explicate my notion of a causal process. This notion is at the centre of my account of agency, and is indeed of more general philosophical importance. For example, I think that the problem of deviant causal chains, as it crops up in epistemology and the philosophy of mind as well as in the philosophy of action, can be solved just with a good account of processes.

My approach to causal explanation, following much of the recent work on the subject, is a two-tier approach (see Salmon 1984: 22). On the one hand, causal explanation is what yields causal understanding; and causal understanding involves having some kind of theoretical model that makes the phenomenon to be explained intelligible. On the other hand, there must be a real causal process which results in the phenomenon. This process is somehow represented by the theoretical model.

I will discuss what sort of thing counts as a theoretical model in Section C. My answer will be a liberal one. I will argue that many different things can take on the role of a theoretical model: a scientific theory consisting of a set of laws and facts, a metaphor, a historical narrative, etc. All that is required is that the model determines a description of what should happen in certain circumstances. The model will be a correct one and so constitute a correct explanation, if and only if it correctly models a causal process which is at work in the world.

I will argue that what is not necessary is that the theoretical model embodies universal truth. I will argue that there is no objection to the descriptions it determines being sometimes false as long as this only happens when the model is applied to situations where the process it represents is not happening.

The other tier concerns the causal determination of the phenomenon to be explained. The position that I am taking here is that an account of causal explanation requires this second tier. This position, which Kim calls 'explanatory realism' is now quite orthodox. It has almost completely taken over from Hempel's single-tier models of explanation which made up the orthodoxy of the 1960s.[1]

According to Hempel's theory of explanation, a good explanation of a phenomenon is a maximally specific, deductively valid, or inductively sound, argument, which involves true universal laws and other true facts, and which concludes that the phenomenon occurs (Hempel 1965).

Hempel's account provides such strong conditions on the theoretical side of explanation that it seems to be able to do without any requirements concerning the actual existence of a causal process. But counter-examples to such an account have been outlined in the philosophical literature since Aristotle. Aristotle, in *Posterior Analytics*, book 2, chapter 16, thought that he could deduce that the moon is eclipsed from the fact that the earth is between the sun and the moon; but he also thought that he could deduce that the earth is between the sun and the moon from the fact that the moon is eclipsed. Only the first of these is explanatory. In the second,

---

[1] Kim (1987), repr. in Ruben (1993: 229). See also Brody (1972), Railton (1978), Achinstein (1981), Salmon (1984), Lewis (1986). For a helpful introduction to the debate on explanation, see Salmon (1989).

although we deduce the less familiar from the more familiar, this is not enough to make the deduction explanatory.

So Hempel's account as it stands seems to be inadequate. But it does not follow that his whole approach is mistaken. One might think that there are certain purely structural constraints on the sorts of arguments that constitute good explanations. Adding such constraints to Hempel's account might deal with the problem of the counter-examples while preserving the spirit of his approach.[2]

The most direct way of characterizing Hempel's approach to explanation is to focus on his insistence that there need be no consideration of actual causal determination in assessing the correctness of an explanation. According to Hempel, it is not to be counted as part of the explanation of the moon's eclipse that it is caused in such-and-such a way. The alternative, explanatory realism, holds that the correctness of an explanation depends on how the phenomenon being explained is causally determined.

Some philosophers think that a reductive account of causal determination can be given in terms of the theoretical side of explanation. Given such a reduction, explanatory realism would be quite compatible with Hempel's approach to explanation. According to explanatory realism, whether or not an explanation is correct depends on the existence of real causal determination. But if there was a reductive account of this causal determination, there would also be an account of what makes an explanation correct without referring to real causal determination.

But there is another sort of counter-example to Hempel's account, which, I think, not only counts against any explanatory non-realist, but also counts against the explanatory realist who believes in a reductive account of causation. This sort of counter-example involves theoretical overdetermination. Achinstein (1981) presents the example of a deductively valid and potentially explanatory argument for the conclusion that Jones dies within twenty-four hours of time t from the premiss that Jones ate a pound of arsenic

---

[2] According to Aristotle, only if deductions stem from definitions of the natures of things are they explanatory. That the earth is between the sun and the moon is part of an account of *what it is* to be an eclipse, but not vice versa. Whether this is anything more than a structural constraint is not clear to me from reading the *Posterior Analytics*. If explanations of particular events are to be grounded in definitions of those particular events in terms of their causal histories, then Aristotle's account goes far beyond Hempel's approach.

at time t and the premiss that anyone who eats a pound of arsenic at time t dies within twenty-four hours of t. However good this argument is, there is nothing in it that rules out the possibility of other arguments for the same conclusion, perhaps involving Jones being run over by a bus at time $t + 1$, say.

If both explanations of Jones dying are equally good as far as their theoretical aspect is concerned and yet only one of them is the correct explanation, then some non-theoretical aspect—presumably the existence of a causal link—will need to be brought in to decide between them. The only way that Hempel's approach can be defended in the light of this is if we can develop some *theoretical* way of ruling out competing explanations.

A natural suggestion is to make the specification of the explanandum so precise that not only are the premisses logically sufficient for the conclusion, but also no alternative set of true premisses is logically sufficient. This might be done by specifying the exact time at which Jones died and by giving more details about the manner of her dying. Such an explanation would be vastly complicated and so would have to be seen as an ideal to which actual explanations may only ever approximate. Also, even the explanandum of such an ideal explanation would not be known by the person seeking the explanation. I might not know exactly how and when Jones died, but still want to find an explanation for why she died.

According to this strategy, for something to be part of an explanation of Jones dying during a certain day, it would have to be part of an ungraspably complicated ideal explanation of a much more precisely specified fact—namely Jones dying at a particular moment in a particular way. I think that there is room to be sceptical as to whether such ideal explanations are even theoretically possible. Even if they were possible, there is something intuitively unsatisfying about saying that strictly speaking we cannot explain Jones dying but only her dying at a certain time in a certain way.

It is important to be clear that I am not arguing that all explanation must be causal explanation. Explaining the meaning of a word or explaining why a certain painting is beautiful is not to be counted as causally explaining anything. Therefore, an account of such explaining need make no reference to causal determination. On the other hand, explaining why something happens is to be counted as causally explaining something.[3] It is my position that an account of such explaining must make reference to causal determination.

More problematic are cases of explaining why something did *not* happen. For example, we might say that Ronald Reagan survived the assassination attempt because the bullet did not hit any vital organs. In some sense this is a causal explanation. But it explains why something (Reagan's death) did not happen by saying that what would have made it happen did not itself happen. It is a difficult question in such cases to decide whether it is right to say that the explanation describes a genuine cause of the thing being explained. If (as I suspect) it is not right to say this, then we have a case of a causal explanation which does not work by describing the cause.

However, it is not clear that such cases should bother an explanatory realist. If it is possible to argue that there is at least a *central* kind of causal explanation which essentially involves describing the cause, then other (negative) kinds of causal explanation can be understood by referring to the central cases.

There are different ways in which the requirement that the correctness of an explanation depends on how the phenomenon to be explained is causally determined may be incorporated into an account of explanation. One very simple way is David Lewis's. According to his account, 'to explain an event is to provide some information about its causal history' (Lewis 1986: 217).

This is to discard every single theoretical constraint on what counts as an explanation. I think that it must be wrong to do this. To say, for example, that something is giving me a headache which once before gave me a headache is not to contribute to an explanation of that headache, though it is to provide information about its causal history.

Another way to be an explanatory realist is to maintain some Hempelian theoretical requirement on what counts as a good explanation and add on an extra requirement that one of the premises of the argument must describe the cause of the phenomenon to be explained. This is Brody's strategy (1972: 23). It makes some kind of attempt at requiring that the theoretical side of an

---

[3] In the next chapter I briefly consider and reject the claim that *teleologically* explaining why something happens is not to be counted as causally explaining it.

explanation represents or describes the causal determination of the event to be explained.

McCarthy (1977) has shown why this strategy as it stands is inadequate. He writes:

> One might suppose that the idea is to mirror the *causal* dependence of *e* [the event to be explained] on its cause by the *deductive* dependence in *d* [the explanatory Deductive-Nomological argument] of a description of *e* upon a description of *e*'s cause. This is an interesting idea; immediately, however, we may begin to suspect a gap in the argument. The basic worry may be put in this way: why should it follow, merely because a D-N derivation of a sentence describing *e* ineliminably involves, *in some way or other*, a description of *e*'s cause that this description functions in the derivation to show (causally) why *e* occurs? No obvious reason exists why a D-N derivation of a sentence describing *e* could not depend on a description of *e*'s cause in some way quite unrelated to the casual dependence of *e* on that cause. (McCarthy 1977: 161)

McCarthy offers the following sort of example of an argument which describes the cause of the event to be explained but nevertheless fails to mirror the causal dependence of the event on its cause.

> *c* is the cause of *e*.
> Either *c* is not the cause of *e* or *e* occurs.
> Therefore *e* occurs.[4]

McCarthy assumes that in order to describe how something happens it is not enough just to describe a cause of it (or even *the* cause of it); one must also describe *how* the phenomenon depends on that cause. This goes far beyond Lewis's account. McCarthy's idea seems to be that by requiring an explanation to involve some *theoretical* determination of a description of the phenomenon it may be possible to represent the *causal* determination of the phenomenon in this wider way. But it is not sufficient that the theoretical determination merely includes a description of the cause; the theoretical determination as a whole must *mirror* the causal determination as a whole.

This is the idea that I will develop in Section D. The key assumption that distinguishes this approach from the usual explanatory realist approaches is that there is more to the description of what makes something happen than a description of the cause; there is

---

[4] This argument needs to be adapted in quite simple ways to satisfy Hempel's requirement of being nomological.

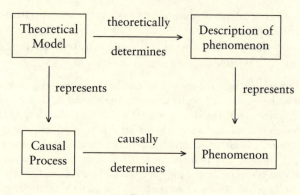

FIGURE 1

also a description of how the phenomenon depends on that cause. Only by describing the causal *process* that results in the phenomenon can one describe this.

Figure 1—the Square of Explanation—represents the account of explanation that is to be developed. My claim is that no part of the square is redundant.

Consider again the example of Jones eating arsenic and being run over by a bus. I suggest that the top half of the Square works just as well for theoretical determination in terms of eating arsenic as it does for theoretical determination in terms of being run over by a bus. So there are two quite different ways in which the description of Jones dying may be determined.

Jones dying is doubly intelligible, but the phenomenon itself is only to be explained in one of these two ways. Which way it is depends on the bottom half of the Square. Each theoretical model represents a possible process—a poisoning-to-death process and a being-run-over-by-a-bus process. Only one of these causally determines the death of Jones. Whichever theoretical model represents the process that causally determines the phenomenon is the true explanation of that phenomenon.

B. PROCESSES

This section treats the bottom half of the Square of Explanation; Section C treats the top half.

A natural picture to have of events and processes is of entities which *extend* through time and which have temporal parts, just as physical objects extend through space and have spatial parts. I want to present an alternative conception of processes as entities which, like physical objects, do not extend in time and do not have temporal parts, but rather *persist* in time.[5] I accept that there are entities—often very closely related entities—which do extend through time and have temporal parts. I will call such entities *events*, and the temporally persisting entities *processes*. I think that this corresponds pretty closely with the way we commonly use these words, but I will not set much store by that.

The starting-point for my way of making the distinction between processes and events is the thought that a *process* is what is described in answer to the question: 'What is/was/will be happening?' An *event*, by contrast, is what is described in answer to the question: 'What happened/will happen/will have happened?' So, the sentence: 'A comet is hurtling into the sun,' describes a process, whereas the sentence: 'A comet hurtled into the sun,' describes an event.

The difference in the two ways that the verb 'to hurtle' is used in these sentences is a difference in what linguists call 'aspect'.[6] The first one has imperfective aspect and the second has perfective aspect. To begin with, I will make it a stipulation concerning my use of the words 'process' and 'event' that processes are associated with descriptions which use the imperfective aspect and events are associated with descriptions which use the perfective aspect. I will go on to argue that this difference in aspect between verbs associated with processes and verbs associated with events corresponds to a distinction in metaphysical categories. The point of making the distinction is to show that processes are not reducible to events.

The first question we need to address is whether it is right to talk about processes as things at all. When I say that an apple is decaying, there is a thing which I am positing, namely the apple. But am I also positing a process, namely the decaying of the apple? There are two equivalent ways of answering the question: 'What is happening?' I can say: 'An apple is decaying,' or I can say: 'The decaying of an apple is happening.' If the second way does not add

---

[5] For a useful discussion of this distinction, see McCann (1979).
[6] The notion of aspect is treated in detail by Comrie (1976) and Galton (1984).

anything to the first, then it looks as though talking about processes as things is quite spurious.

However, a strong prima-facie case can be made for treating processes as particular things. Consider the process of a bush fire spreading through the countryside. Suppose I see a bush fire spreading through one bit of woodland and then some time later see a bush fire spreading through another bit. There is one sense in which it is fairly obvious that what is happening in each case is the same thing—namely a bush fire spreading through the woodland. But there is a further question which we may be interested in, and which is naturally expressed by asking whether it is the very same process of fire spreading which is observed on both occasions.

So, there is room for a type–token distinction in describing processes; the type being that of a bush fire spreading, and the token being that of this particular bush fire spreading. There might be different token processes of bush fire spreading which all belong to the same type of process. Given this distinction, we should be able to find identity conditions for token processes across time— conditions under which this particular bush fire spreading is the very same as that one.

In the end, I think that the question of whether it is right to claim the existence of such things depends on whether there is a way of identifying and reidentifying them. This depends on a broadly Strawsonian approach to metaphysics (P. Strawson 1959), which I adopt without trying to defend. For the time being I just want to give the benefit of the doubt to the view that processes are particulars. But I think that my treatment does provide the basis for constructing identity conditions for processes.

The next question to answer is whether processes and events are distinct entities. For example, we describe the decaying of an apple as a process—i.e. as something that is/was/will be happening. But sometimes we might also describe the decaying of an apple as an event—i.e. as something that has happened/will have happened/etc. We might say that the process of the apple decaying has been going on for over two weeks now. But we might also say that the event of the apple decaying was what spurred me into a study of biochemical reactions in fruit. Is the process of the apple decaying—what was happening—the same thing as the event of the apple decaying—what happened? I think that the answer is clearly, no.

We want to say at one stage of the apple's decay that the very same process was going on as was going on at an earlier stage. This single process cannot be identified with the event of the apple decaying. For suppose that something interfered with the process so that the later stage never happened—perhaps the half-rotten apple was put into deep-freeze. This would not affect the identity of the process at the earlier stage before the interference. What was happening before the interference is not affected by whether or not the interference occurred. But the event, i.e. what happened, is affected by whether or not the apple is put into deep-freeze. The event that happened before the interference is not the same as the whole event without the interference. So the process and the event cannot be literally identical.

The conclusion that a process such as that of an apple decaying is not identical with the associated event of an apple decaying may seem obviously wrong. After all, nothing more is needed before it is right to say that the event has happened than that the process has stopped happening. There is nothing more to the event than the completed happening of the process. But this does not contradict my conclusion. What I am arguing is that a process should not be identified with its completed happening. Really, they belong to quite different logical categories. They should no more be equated than should, say, a human being and the life of that human being.

This is so even for processes whose descriptions mention their completion; for example the process of walking to the shop or the process of a comet hurtling into the sun. The same argument can show that the process of walking to the shop is distinct from the event of walking to the shop, and that the process of a comet hurtling into the sun is distinct from the event of the comet hurtling into the sun.

Processes, however they are described, can always be interrupted. What it is for a process to be interrupted is for it to be happening and then for something to stop it happening before it has reached completion, or before it would otherwise have ended. This interruption does not mean that it was not happening before the interruption. I am walking to the shop and on the way get arrested by the police. What was happening before I got arrested was that I was walking to the shop. It is the same thing that would have been happening later if I had been allowed to reach the shop. But what *happened* before I got arrested (i.e. the event) was not the same as what would have happened if I had not been arrested. There is some event in common between the two cases, namely the event of my walking as far as the policeman. But what is not common between the two cases is the event of my walking to the shop.

Exactly the same argument shows that a process cannot be literally identical with the series of its stages, where the stages might be thought of as states of affairs, events, or even sub-processes. It does not really make sense to say that the series of stages constituting my progress to the shop is interrupted. The series of stages up to the point of arrest was not interrupted; it was completed. The series of stages including the stage of my reaching the shop never occurred, and so it cannot have been interrupted either.

Although it is wrong to identify a process with the sum of its stages, the stages of a process are essential to it in some sense. Although particular stages are not essential to a particular process, that what is going on is a process of a certain kind—e.g. of an apple decaying—requires a certain kind of *structure* of stages to occur. There is a certain characteristic structure of changes that constitutes decay; the process of an apple decaying is not happening unless changes are occurring which belong to that characteristic structure. (Given the argument against identifying a process with a series of stages, it is important that such a structure of stages is not so rigidly specified that interruptions to a process are ruled out.)

There are two accounts of processes taking off from this point which I would like to consider. One, which I shall call the Russellian account, regards the satisfaction of the appropriate structural principle by a series of stages to be *all* that is required for a process of a certain kind to be happening. The other, which I shall call the Aristotelian account, accepts that some structural principle will be satisfied by the constituent stages of a process, but insists that all that is required for a certain kind of process to be happening is that some underlying nature be continuously present.

In *The Physics* (201^a10-11) Aristotle wrote that 'the fulfilment of what exists potentially, in so far as it exists potentially, is motion.' I will interpret this for my own purposes to mean that a process is the realization of those features which, taken together, constitute the underlying conditions for a certain structure of changes. (I do not mean the word 'realization' to carry any implication of becoming realized, but to mean simply that the features *are* realized.) So a process of alteration is the realization of those conditions which constitute the underlying conditions for that alteration. The process of an apple decaying is the realization of whatever conditions constitute the underlying nature of the series of changes associated with an apple decaying.

My interpretation of Aristotle may seem strange since the word Aristotle uses for motion in this passage is *kinesis* and yet the notion of a process that I am trying to extract may seem closer to Aristotle's use of the word *energeia*. I am not at all sure whether this means that there is anything wrong with my interpretation as an interpretation of Aristotle. But, in any case, I will shelter behind the phrase 'Aristotelian account' and remain neutral about Aristotle's own account.[7]

So, according to my interpretation of the Aristotelian account of processes, there are two requirements for the happening of a process. The first requirement is that there is some set of conditions constituting the underlying nature of some characteristic series of stages. These conditions constitute the 'potentiality' for this characteristic series of stages. The second requirement is that these conditions be fulfilled. This is all there is to the presence of a process. What this means is that on any particular occasion of identifying a process as happening one does not have to identify the characteristic series of stages, as long as one has already identified what conditions are *in general* sufficient for that series of stages. One need only identify that such conditions are indeed at present fulfilled.

According to the Russellian account, on the other hand, what is required in order to tell that a certain process is happening is to determine that a certain kind of series of stages occurs. Russell (1903: sect. 442) says that 'Motion is the occupation by one entity, of a continuous series of places at a continuous series of times.'[8] Extending this to processes generally, we might say that a process of a certain kind occurs if a continuous temporally extended series of stages of a thing or things satisfies some structural principle which determines that they belong to that kind.

This Russellian account, as I am presenting it, is about the requirements that need to be satisfied for it to be true that a process

---

[7] My thinking about processes has been largely influenced by Charles (1984: ch. 1), though he certainly does not accept that my Aristotelian account is exactly Aristotle's account.

[8] Salmon's 'at-at' account of processes (1984) is an example of a more modern account which endorses Russell's claim.

of a certain kind is happening, and is not automatically committed to the view, rejected earlier, that a particular process is to be identified with a particular series of events. (I suspect that Russell himself was committed to that view, however.) We could say that nothing more is required for the existence of a process of some sort than that a certain kind of series of stages occurs, while allowing the identity conditions for a particular process to differ from those for a series of stages. A Russellian might express this by claiming that a process is to be identified with a *structure* of stages, rather than with a series of stages. One and the same structure of stages might be realized by different particular series of stages. For example, the structure of stages involved in the apple's completely decaying should count as the same as the structure of stages involved in the apple's decaying up to the point of being put into deep-freeze. The two structures have their initial stages in common and they each satisfy the appropriate structural constraints constitutive of apple decaying.

Only certain kinds of structures of stages may constitute processes. For example, if the stages are chaotically disconnected, then there is no process which is the happening of these stages. The blinking of my eye followed ten minutes later by a snowflake falling on the South Pole followed ten years later by a light being switched off in New York does not count as a process happening. So a Russellian account should include a specification of the sorts of structures of stages which may count as processes. Russell, at least in the case of motion, requires that there should be continuity between the stages of a process. But allowing only continuous structures of stages to count as processes may be too limiting when we move away from the case of motion. Indeed, when we consider other sorts of processes, it is not at all clear how to construe the notion of continuity.

I would like to say that what geologists call the freeze–thaw process of erosion is really a process. Here, water gets into the cracks of rocks, freezes overnight, thus widening the cracks, and then thaws in the morning. The following night, or perhaps in the following few nights, water gets into the cracks again, freezes, and widens the cracks still further. After a certain amount of crack-widening, the stresses in the rock become too much and bits of rock shear off and are washed away. After a large-enough number of repetitions of this, the rock has become significantly eroded.

When the rock dries out during the day, the freeze–thaw process is still happening. If the Russellian account is going to keep the requirement of temporal continuity, then it must treat such dormant spells as part of the structure of stages of the process, despite the fact that such spells contribute nothing to the process. It would have to say that a freeze–thaw process is happening if a freeze episode is in progress, a thaw episode is progress, or an episode between such episodes is in progress.

By filling in the temporal gaps between stages with dormant spells which also count as stages, the Russellian account can preserve some requirement of continuity. This requirement is that of temporal rather than of spatio-temporal continuity; indeed, I am not sure that the notion of spatio-temporal continuity makes much sense in the context of this sort of process. But temporal continuity is an easy, perhaps all too easy, requirement to satisfy. However chaotic and disconnected a structure of stages is, it can be made temporally continuous just by filling in the temporal gaps with dormant stages.

One rather un-Russellian direction for the Russellian account to take here is to give a more Aristotelian construction of the notion of continuity. It might say that different stages are continuous in a process if there is some common causal ground, or, perhaps, spatio-temporally continuous causal ground, for the different stages. The continuous presence of such a causal ground would ensure that the structure of stages formed a causal unity.

By including the requirement that the structure of stages forms a causal unity in this sort of way, the Russellian account would be moving closer to the Aristotelian account. But, as long as the Russellian account is committed to *identifying* a process with such a structure of stages, it remains distinct from the Aristotelian account. In the Aristotelian account, the identification of a process does not depend on the identification of a structure of stages, but rather depends on the identification of the underlying set of conditions for such a structure of stages.

The distinction between these two accounts is quite subtle, but there is a metaphysical claim about processes which I think we should hold on to, and which is only accommodated by the hardline Aristotelian account. The claim is that at any one moment when a process is happening, what is happening is the whole process, not just part of it. In the Russellian account, which identifies a process with a certain kind of structure of stages, the stages must be thought of as temporal parts of the process. The process consists of these stages and extends over the duration of the structure. What is present at any one time then cannot be the whole process, because for the whole process to be present all its parts must be present, and the stages that have not yet happened are not present.

The Aristotelian account, by contrast, does not identify a process with a structure of stages; and so there is no need in this account to think of its stages as temporal parts. At any one moment the process as a whole can be identified since its underlying nature can be identified. This allows one to think of the process as persisting through time rather than being extended in time. The stages of a process do not constitute it, but should be thought of rather as manifestations of the process happening.

The claim that what is happening at any one moment when the process is happening is the whole process not just part of it follows from being able to identify what is happening now with what was happening before and indeed with what is happening at all times during the course of the process. If what is happening now were just a temporal part of the process then it would not be identical with what is happening at another time since that will be a different temporal part. So, what is happening now must be the whole thing.

It is very easy to get confused about this. Although in one sense what is happening is the same at every stage of a process, other things are happening which may vary. For example, at every stage of the process of the rock undergoing freeze–thaw erosion one thing is happening which remains the same thing throughout, namely that process of freeze–thaw erosion itself. But also different things are happening—water is getting into a crack, water is freezing in a crack, the crack is expanding, and so on. The stages of a process may be thought of as states, as instantaneous changes of state, as events, or as sub-processes themselves. The latter possibility is what leads to the confusion, for then there are alternative ways of answering the question: 'What is happening?' We might say that the main process is happening, in which case what is happening is the same throughout the course of the process. Or we might say that the sub-process is happening, in which case what is happening differs as the process progresses. The point to hold on to is that, although different things may be happening throughout the course of a process, there is something happening at every moment of the process which is the same, namely the process itself. This is what is required for the claim under consideration, which is that what is happening at any moment during a process is the whole process, not just part of it.

This is denied by Gareth Evans in his exchange with Peter Strawson concerning the identification of sound sequences (although, to be fair to Evans, there is no indication that he would deny this for processes generally).

If the concept of reidentification is to be used in connection with processes, it must be understood that it is being used in a different sense from that which it has in connection with things. We reidentify a process when we hold that an occurrence encountered at one time is part of the same process encountered at another, but it is a distinctive (and some have thought incoherent) feature of our conceptual scheme of material bodies that we suppose an object to be both present as a whole on one occasion, and literally identical with an object present as a whole on another. (Evans 1985: 257–8)

But the claim that what is present at any moment is not the whole process but only a process-part is already an admission of defeat if one's aim is to capture a common-sense notion of processes. It is every bit as bad as the parallel claim that an object as a whole is not present at any one moment, but all that is present is a time-slice of an object. For it is also a distinctive feature of our conceptual scheme of processes that we suppose a process to be both present as a whole on one occasion and literally identical with a process present as a whole on another. The phrase, 'what is happening now', is naturally taken to denote a whole process; and we *do* want to claim that what is happening now is literally identical with what is happening at some other time.

It seems to me that what Evans has in mind in that quotation is not the process in my sense—the thing that is happening—but the event which is the completion of the process. This event is something which extends rather than persists, and is reidentified in just the way that Evans suggests. The Russellian account of processes combined with the more Aristotelian conception of continuity works perfectly well as an account of such events. In most of what follows, the distinction between a process and the event which is the completion of that process is not particularly significant. But since, according to my view, the process is the more fundamental of the two, I will continue to try to make sense of the hardline Aristotelian conception of processes.

What may seem puzzling about the hardline Aristotelian account is that while maintaining that the fulfilment of the appropriate underlying conditions is both necessary and sufficient for a process to be happening, it also accepts that it is necessary in order for a process to be happening that its characteristic structure of stages occurs. What about the apparent possibility that the underlying conditions are fulfilled but that the characteristic structure of stages fails to materialize? What is the Aristotelian going to say if all the appropriate underlying conditions of the process of an apple decaying are satisfied, but no decay occurs. The Aristotelian account might appear to define this possibility out of existence; yet defining possibilities out of existence is obviously fallacious.

This would be a problem for the Aristotelian account if the account was both defining as a necessary condition of a certain process occurring that a certain structure, S, of stages occurs, and defining as a sufficient condition of the same process occurring that certain underlying conditions, C, are realized. It would follow from such a definition as a necessary truth that if conditions C are realized, stages S occur. Clearly such a substantial conclusion should not be allowed to follow from a mere definition.

But in fact the Aristotelian account does not incorporate such a fallacy. The account does not define as sufficient for any particular process to be happening that a *particular* set of conditions, C, is realized. Rather, what is defined as sufficient is that the set of conditions, whatever it is, which underlies a certain structure of stages is realized. Given any particular set of conditions, such a definition does not rule out the possibility of the characteristic stages of the process failing to materialize.

According to the Aristotelian account which I have been defending, we may say that there are two conditions which must be satisfied if a process which is characterized by a certain structure of stages is happening:

(i) there is a set of underlying conditions for that structure of stages;

(ii) that set of conditions is realized.

It seems natural to suppose that for a set of conditions to constitute the underlying nature of a certain structure of stages such conditions must be *sufficient* for the structure of stages to occur. Whenever the set of underlying conditions is realized the structure of stages necessarily follows. This is because, according to the Aristotelian account, when the underlying conditions hold true the process must be happening; and when the process is happening its characteristic stages must occur.

This may look like a very strong claim. It seems to rule out the possibility of processes going wrong for one reason or another—either because they are interfered with or because of some failure in determinism due to quantum-level randomness. But it is very important to make a distinction between two ways in which processes might be thought to go wrong according to the Aristotelian account. The first way is that the underlying conditions might fail to persist, thus ending the process. The second way is that while the underlying conditions persist the characteristic stages might fail to materialize. It is only the second of these which is at issue when considering the question of whether to require that the persistence of underlying conditions should necessitate the occurrence of the characteristic stages.

In line with this distinction, two different kinds of interference with processes may be distinguished. The first kind is when something interferes with the underlying conditions of a process, so that they no longer obtain, and the characteristic stages of the process consequently fail to follow. The second kind is when the underlying conditions are not interfered with, but the characteristic stages are directly affected by some interference which prevents them from taking place.

The first kind of interference is what would have happened to the freeze–thaw process if a meteorite knocked the earth out of its usual orbit and brought about a change in climate. Such a possibility does not threaten the claim that while the underlying conditions of a process hold, the characteristic stages must occur. For after this kind of interference the underlying conditions can no longer be said to hold. The second sort of interference is more threatening. As an example of this, consider the process of the sun warming up a stone being interfered with by a cold wind blowing over the stone at exactly the same time, thus cancelling out the effect. It seems that the underlying conditions of the process of the sun warming up the stone may be in place while the characteristic stages fail to occur.

One response that one might make to this example on behalf of the Aristotelian account would be to require of underlying conditions that the structure of stages necessarily follows *unless something interferes*. But a better response would be to include the conditions that constitute non-interference as part of the underlying nature of a process. This is because when a certain process is interfered with we want to say that the process is not happening, rather than say that it is happening but failing to result in its characteristic stages.

It is wrong to say either that the sun is heating up the stone or that the wind is cooling down the stone. Something is lacking in the underlying conditions of both processes; in the case of the warming-up process this would be some fact about the temperature of the air around the stone. This is not to say that nothing is happening in this case. For example, the sun is stopping the stone from cooling down and the wind is stopping the stone from heating up. These are two processes whose underlying conditions are fully realized. Alternatively, we might talk of the process of the sun making the stone warmer than it would otherwise have been.

So the possibility of interference need not threaten the claim that the persisting presence of the underlying conditions of a process is sufficient for the occurrence of the characteristic stages of that process. Another thing which may be thought to threaten this claim is the apparent possibility of indeterministic processes in quantum physics. But different sorts of cases need to be distinguished here, too. First, there are cases of the failure of the underlying conditions due to quantum-level randomness. An example of this is given by Railton.

It might seem a fine explanation for a light's going out that we opened the only circuit connecting it with an electrical source, but an element of chance was involved: had enough atoms in the vicinity of the light undergone spontaneous beta-decay at the right moment, the electrons emitted could have kept it glowing. (1978: 132)

The fact that massive spontaneous beta-decay is not happening in the vicinity of the light should be counted as part of the underlying nature of the process of the light going off. The possibility of this underlying condition failing to hold does not show that there is a possibility of the characteristic stages of a process failing to occur given the presence of the underlying conditions. What would be needed to show this would be a case of indeterminacy in the result of a process rather than of indeterminacy in the conditions of a process.

The sort of case that might be thought to exemplify indeterminacy in the results of a process is the following. Consider the event of an electron in an interference-split experiment being registered by one particular detector in a battery of detectors. Let us assume the Copenhagen interpretation of quantum theory, according to which, *nothing* determines that it should be this particular detector rather than any of the others that registers the electron. But I do not think that it follows from this that this event is the indeterministic result of some process. There is a quantum-mechanical process one of whose stages is that there is such-and-such a probability of that event occurring. But the quantum-mechanical process stops there; it does not go on to make the event happen. The whole point about indeterministic events is that nothing makes them happen.[9]

So I do think that there is no good reason to deny that something only counts as the underlying nature of a process if its continuous presence necessitates the occurrence of the characteristic stages of that process. But what now of the question of whether there is some sense in which the presence of the underlying nature of a process at some time necessitates the occurrence of the characteristic stages of the process at later times?

This may be incorporated into an account of processes by requiring of underlying conditions that they are naturally persisting. It is too much to require simply that the presence of underlying conditions necessitates their continued presence. Other processes may happen whose characteristic stages involve changes to the underlying nature of a process. This is what happens when the underlying conditions are interfered with. So the most that we could require is that underlying conditions persist if nothing interferes with them. Perhaps the possibility of extremely unlikely random quantum-mechanical events, like the massive spontaneous beta-decay considered by Railton, means that this is still too strong. Then we would have to require that underlying conditions were such that their presence at a particular time necessitated the high probability of their continued presence at a later time so long as nothing interfered with them. Given this restriction on what counts as the underlying nature of a process, a process is indeed a thing whose correct

---

[9] See Kitcher (1989) for similar claims.

identification has implications, albeit hypothetical and perhaps probabilistic, for the future.

The requirement that underlying conditions are naturally persisting might be found puzzling given the thought that in complex processes whose stages develop over time there must be something dynamic about the underlying nature of the process to keep track of which stage has been reached. According to this thought the underlying nature of such processes must include features described by dummy variables whose values change as the process develops. But this is not really a puzzle. For rather than having the value of such dummy variables in the underlying conditions, some higher-order invariant property of the dummy variables should be included.

I think that a proper treatment of the notion of underlying conditions would have to be a lot more detailed, and here I am really only gesturing at what would be involved. For example, perhaps a further condition on the set of underlying conditions is that the set should include no redundant conditions. Suppose I add to a set of sufficient conditions for an apple decaying the condition that the moon is full. The new set of conditions is still sufficient for the characteristic structure of stages, but it seems quite wrong to say that there is a special full-moon apple-decaying process distinct from the non-full-moon apple-decaying process. So perhaps instead one should require that the set of underlying conditions be the *minimal* sufficient set of conditions.

According to the Aristotelian account, a process is the realization of those conditions that constitute the potentiality for a certain structure of stages. I have been interpreting this claim in such a way that what it is for a set of conditions to be realized is just for them to hold true. So there is no gap between the potentiality being present and its being realized in a process. There is no room here for the possibility of unfulfilled potentialities.

This notion of a potentiality fails to capture our (or indeed Aristotle's) notion of a capacity. For, unless we are actualists, we want to allow that something may have a certain capacity without that capacity being fulfilled in a process.[10] In other words, there should be a distinction between the holding true of the conditions which constitute a capacity and the activation of that capacity. The activation involves the satisfaction of further conditions.

---

[10] Actualism is the doctrine that only the actual is real—there are no possibilities beyond the ones which are realized.

Room can be made for such a distinction in my account. First, let me stipulate a distinction between realization and activation. A capacity is *realized* if the conditions which constitute or underlie that capacity hold true. This just means that the capacity is fully present. A capacity is *activated* if those further conditions are realized which turn the capacity into a process. Then, let me distinguish between the technical notion of potentiality that figures in the Aristotelian account of processes and the common-sense notion of capacity. A potentiality is such that if all its conditions hold true, then the respective process is happening. A capacity is such that it may be present and yet, until it is activated, the respective process is not happening.

A car might have the capacity to go at 100 m.p.h. even when it is in the garage and not in the process of going at 100 m.p.h. But, if the complete potentiality for the car going at 100 m.p.h. is present, then the car is going at 100 m.p.h. If a capacity is activated, then it becomes a complete potentiality. In this case, activation consists in getting the car on the open road with the engine running, the throttle down, in top gear, fuel in the tank, etc.

According to the way I am presenting the Aristotelian account, the conditions underlying the characteristic stages of some process constitute the potentiality for that process. These conditions can then be divided between those conditions which constitute a capacity for that process and those which constitute the activation of that capacity. How this division should be made does not need to be considered in order to determine whether or not such a process is happening, since that only depends on the realization of the underlying nature. If this is right, then the notion of a process can be understood prior to that of a capacity.

Now, we do not usually talk of a situation having a capacity, rather we talk of an object, or, more generally, a persisting entity, having a capacity. So, in order to attribute a capacity, it must be possible to identify a persisting, self-standing, entity within the underlying conditions of a process. Let me call such an entity a *mechanism* for that process. If we can identify such a mechanism, then we can say that it has the capacity either to undergo or to cause the characteristic stages of that process. And, we can say that it has this capacity whether or not the other conditions hold. This is the point of requiring that a mechanism is self-standing; one can attribute a capacity without committing oneself to its activation.

As it stands, this is a slightly eccentric use of the word 'capacity'. For it follows that not only is a watch a mechanism with the capacity to enable someone to tell the time, but so is a watch-spring; not only has a car got the capacity to travel at 100 m.p.h., but so has the distributor unit. To mark this eccentricity, let me call such capacities, 'theoretical capacities'. It does not sound so wrong to say that a watch-spring has the theoretical capacity to enable someone to tell the time. All you need to do to activate this theoretical capacity is to combine the spring with all the other parts of a watch in the right way.

According to the more natural way of talking about capacities, we would say that the watch-spring does not have the capacity to enable someone to tell the time. We would say this because it is not a practical possibility for most of us to activate the watch-spring in the right way. Let me call this sort of capacity, a 'practical capacity'. A car without petrol in its tank may still have the practical capacity to travel at 100 m.p.h. But a car without an engine under its bonnet, although it has that theoretical capacity, does not have that practical capacity.[11]

C. UNDERSTANDING

Now I consider what constraints there must be on the theoretical side of an explanation. First of all, as many philosophers have remarked, the notion of a good explanation is a pragmatic one (see van Fraassen 1980 and Achinstein 1983). An answer to a why-question only constitutes a good explanation if it is a useful answer. To see this consider some answers which, in standard contexts, are not useful.

Question: Why did the chicken cross the road?
Answer: Because its little legs kept pumping up and down.

Question: Why did the apple fall from the tree?
Answer: Because it couldn't very well fall from anything else, since it started off being attached to the tree.

---

[11] It is this notion of a practical capacity that Ayers is discussing (1968: ch. 5). He attempts to capture the difference between the condition of the car having an engine and the condition of the car having fuel as a difference between intrinsic and extrinsic conditions. But this distinction in turn seems to depend on practical considerations.

The first answer is not useful, because the questioner probably wanted a different kind of explanation—a teleological one that specified why it was in the interest of the chicken to cross the road. Van Fraassen calls that part of the context of the question which determines the kind of explanation that is being sought the *relevance relation*. The second answer is not useful because it assumes the wrong contrast in the question. The questioner probably wanted to know why the apple fell from the tree rather than stayed in the tree. The questioner probably did not want to know why the apple fell from the tree rather than from anything else. Van Fraassen calls this second aspect of the context of a question its *contrast class*.

As Achinstein (1983) notes, if these contextual aspects can be specified in the question, then this pragmatic aspect does not force us to provide a relativistic account of good explanation. If the question is just 'Why did the chicken cross the road?' then what constitutes a good answer is relative to the questioner. But if the explanandum is expanded to make the contextual features explicit, then this is not so obvious. So if the question is 'Given such-and-such relevance relation and contrast class, why did the chicken cross the road?' then perhaps we can evaluate the answer independently of any consideration of the state of the questioner.

Achinstein himself does not feel confident that this can be done, however. The notion of a good explanation that we are after is that of an *appropriate* response to the question. According to Achinstein, the notion of appropriateness cannot be spelt out explicitly without referring to the state of the audience. Given this, an account of the notion of a good explanation must be relativistic. For example Boyle's Law was a good explanation of the behaviour of gas at the time and given his audience, but now and given the current scientific community, it is not a good explanation.

We might agree that the notion of a good explanation is relativistic, but think that there is a slimmed-down notion of a *scientifically correct* explanation that is not relativistic. Achinstein rejects this possibility also (1983: ch. 5). His argument here is by inspection and rejection of the existing attempts to specify such a notion. He concludes that 'there seems to be no non-arbitrary standard of minimal scientific correctness based on some particular subset of methodological values' (1983: 192). This argument from exhaustion of the current accounts leaves open the possibility of finding a new account which is successful. I shall attempt to find one here.

If Achinstein is right and there is no satisfactory objective way of assessing explanations, then the consequences are quite serious. Either we must rest content with relativistic ways of assessing explanations or we must follow David Lewis (1986) and give up any pragmatic constraints on the notion of explanation, allowing any information about the causal history of a phenomenon to be part of an explanation of it. Either of these is disastrous for anyone who wants to give a philosophical account of anything in terms of whether it is explained in a certain way (for example, the Teleological Theory of Action). According to the first possibility, the account will fail to provide an objective notion. On the second possibility, the account will fail to provide any constraints.

The primary point of an explanation is to provide understanding. An account of understanding, or at least some scientifically minimal sort of understanding, should lead into an account of explanation. Also, by starting with understanding, we can distinguish two separate possible sources of relativity in the notion of a correct explanation. The first is that the notion of understanding itself might be ineliminably relative, i.e. there might be no way of describing what is involved in understanding something which is constant for different people. The second is that the account of correct explanation in terms of understanding might be ineliminably relativistic, i.e. there might be no way of describing what is involved in a good way to provide understanding which is constant for different people.

I will start with the thought that understanding why some phenomenon occurs involves knowing about the causal process that results in that phenomenon. This does not commit me to the thought that all understanding is causal, but just that there is an important sort of understanding which is. The question of this section is what sort of knowledge of the causal process constitutes this causal understanding.

There are two quite different kinds of knowledge that can both be described as knowledge of the process that results in some phenomenon. Let me describe these respectively as superficial and underlying knowledge. Superficial knowledge is knowledge of the characteristic stages of a process resulting in the phenomenon and of how that phenomenon fits into those characteristic stages. Underlying knowledge is knowledge of the underlying nature of the process resulting in the phenomenon and of why that underlying nature has the characteristic stages it does.

As an illustration, consider the process of a computer adding the input numbers 3 and 5 to output the number 8. Knowledge of this process may concern the characteristic results of the process, or it may concern why the process has those characteristic results. So there are two quite different kinds of answer to the question of how the process works:

1. If two numbers are input, their sum will be output.
2. There is present an electrical configuration corresponding to such-and-such a computer program.

The first way describes the characteristic results of the process, while the second way describes the underlying structure of the process. (Clearly there will be more or less detailed ways of doing the second of these.)

What does one need to know in order to understand why the number 8 was output by the computer? First of all, one should know that the event was the result of a process whose characteristic stages are described by (1) above. This means that one must know how to describe the characteristic stages of that process, and one must know that the event results from a process so characterized.

Accompanying the knowledge of what the characteristic stages are, one should have knowledge of how the process worked in this particular instance. In other words, one should know how the phenomenon—the number 8 being output—fits into the characteristic type of event structure of the process that results in it. In this example one need only know that the numbers 3 and 5 were input and that 8 represents their sum.

Knowledge of how a process that results in some phenomenon works in general and did work in particular to result in that phenomenon constitutes what I am calling superficial knowledge of why that phenomenon occurred. Such knowledge need not depend on any ability to identify that process reliably through its underlying and abiding nature. I might have complete superficial knowledge of why the number 8 was output if I have simply been told that the computer is outputting the sum of its inputs which were 3 and 5. To be able to identify that process through its underlying nature requires knowledge of computer science. Such ability is part of the underlying knowledge of the process.

When I just have superficial knowledge concerning why the number 8 was output, there may be further questions that I want answered. I may want to know what the underlying nature of the process with those characteristic stages is, and I may want to know why that underlying nature results in such stages. If I do not have this extra underlying knowledge, then I do not understand the process resulting in the phenomenon. I know what the process is, but I do not know why it works the way it does. So, without superficial knowledge, I may know what the phenomenon is but not why it occurs. Similarly, without underlying knowledge, I may know what the process resulting in the phenomenon is, but not why it works the way it does.

This suggests that we should not require that underlying knowledge is necessary in order to understand why a phenomenon happens, but only that it is necessary in order to understand why something else, namely the process resulting in the phenomenon, happens. If I know that 3 and 5 were input into an adding process then I have complete understanding of why 8 was output. But this does not give me any understanding of why an adding process was happening. For this I need underlying knowledge.

So, I want to claim that there is an important sense in which we can have complete understanding of why something happens just by having the superficial knowledge—knowledge of what the characteristic stages are of a process which results in that thing happening. A scientist will not be happy with only having this sort of understanding. In particular, they will want to understand why the process has the characteristic stages that it does have. But it is important to see that this involves answering a quite different question to the question of why the thing happened.

It should be pointed out that underlying knowledge does not automatically provide one with superficial knowledge. I may know all about the workings of a computer and its program, but still not understand why a certain number is output if I do not know what was input. So, having deeper knowledge does not mean that one can do without the superficial knowledge if one wants to know why something occurs.

Obviously, if there were no such thing as processes, then this superficial level of knowledge would not exist either. One would have to rely on the theoretical aspects of explanation. In this case, complete understanding could only be had when the theoretical way of telling what should happen was perfect. This would not be exhausted by the knowledge that I have characterized as superficial. So, this account of understanding depends on some account of processes, like the one in Section B, being possible.

Similarly, suppose that there were such a thing as processes but that they were metaphysically reducible to progressively finer-grained processes. By this I mean that there is a token identity between a process and the set of its sub-processes. Then it would only be a convenient way of speaking to say that a certain macro-level process was happening. It would be more complete to say that a certain pattern of subatomic processes was happening. In this case, knowledge of the characteristic events of the macro-level process could not be part of the real understanding of why the phenomenon occurs.

My response to this is that one should resist the thought that the process of a candle burning down is metaphysically reducible to a structure of subatomic processes, just as one should resist the thought that the candle itself is metaphysically reducible to a structure of subatomic particles. It is just not the case that these entities are identified in terms of these sub-entities. So it is always possible for the same process to consist of different sub-processes. As long as the underlying essential nature of a process is continuously present and its characteristic stages occur, variation in the sub-processes is possible. This means that a token-identity cannot be set up between a process and its sub-processes.

Another argument goes as follows. Even without metaphysical reduction, it is still true that we can describe the world in terms of more and more basic processes. The more basic the processes that we have in our world-picture the more accurate is that picture. So explaining anything in terms of the characteristic events of macro-level processes is made scientifically redundant by underlying knowledge of how the world may be described in terms of the finer-grained processes.

However, there are two good reasons why superficial knowledge is not made scientifically redundant by underlying knowledge. The first is that macro-level *phenomena* can only be accounted for by reference to macro-level processes, unless the macro-level phenomena are themselves metaphysically reducible to fine-grained phenomena. Assuming that the phenomenon of a rabbit eating a blade of grass cannot be identified with some micro-level event-structure, then any explanation at the subatomic level will fail to explain *it*.

The second reason is that, even if macro-level phenomena could be reduced to fine-grained phenomena, the information required to make a fine-grained explanation may be practically inaccessible, whereas that required to achieve understanding on the macro-level is available. Even if it were the case that by knowing the position, velocity, etc., of every particle in a closed system one could explain some macro-level phenomenon occurring in that system, practically achievable explanation of that phenomenon in terms of superficial knowledge would be at no risk of being made redundant. It may be that a main interest of science is in investigating and understanding the fundamental nature of processes rather than in just investigating how they work (i.e. what their results are). But this does not make redundant every other kind of investigation and understanding.

In conclusion, there is a level of understanding which is provided by knowledge of the characteristic stages of a process resulting in a phenomenon and of how that phenomenon fits into these characteristic stages. It is appropriate to describe this as understanding why the phenomenon occurs. In terms of just this kind of understanding, nothing is lacking if underlying knowledge of the mechanism is lacking. This underlying knowledge is part of understanding something else altogether—i.e. why the process has the characteristic stages it does. This latter kind of understanding does not make the former more superficial kind of understanding redundant.

There may be a suspicion that the requirement of superficial knowledge is too *strong* a requirement for understanding. For to know what the characteristic stages of a process are one must know what the different results of that process are in different circumstances. One may understand full well why 8 was output by the computer when 3 and 5 were input, yet not be good enough at arithmetic to know what the characteristic output will be when 2,639 and 401,921 are input. However, I think this sort of case proves nothing. For at least one knows that the sum of 2,639 and 401,921 will be the characteristic output.

A more interesting case is the following. Suppose that the computer has been programmed to add all input pairs except the pair 2,639 and 401,921, which it multiplies. Is it not unnecessarily tough to demand that knowledge of this exceptional case is required before one can understand all the other quite separate cases?

In fact, this case reveals the strength of my account. Most computer programs designed to have such output would work with two separate modules, one for adding the inputs and another for multiplying them together. A third module would be used for passing control to one of the other two depending on whether or not the inputs were 2,639 and 401,921. In a computer so programmed there would be an identifiable mechanism underlying a process that characteristically resulted in the sum of its inputs. It would be possible to identify this mechanism and hence the process quite separately from the rest of the system.

The event of 8 being output is the result of the adding process alone as well as simultaneously being the result of the combined adding and multiplying process. These processes are neither independent of each other nor identical to each other. They happen at the same time, to the same things, and with the same results. But they are as distinct from one another as are a plant and its stem or a house and its walls.

If one knows about one of the processes—the simple adding process—and not the other, then one understands why 8 was output in virtue of that. It is not a requirement of this sort of understanding that one knows about all the processes that result in the phenomenon. Nor is it a requirement that one knows exactly in what circumstances the process that one does know about is happening. One need only know that it is happening in this case, how it works when it does happen, and how the phenomenon fits into this. So, not knowing about the fact that this adding process does not happen when 2,639 and 401,921 are input does not detract from one's understanding.

However, suppose that the computer program is not separable in this way. Suppose that it is impossible to identify a separate mechanism which always adds when it works properly. Then, in this case, one does not understand why 8 is output when 3 and 5 are input. For the output is not the result of adding the inputs, but of a more complicated function that happens to give the same results as adding for all numbers except 2,639 and 401,921. In this case, failure to know what should be the output when 2,639 and 401,921 are input shows a failure to understand what process it is that determines that 8 is output when 3 and 5 are input.

So it seems reasonable after all to assume that one must know what the results are of a process which determines the occurrence of the phenomenon to be understood in *all* circumstances within the proper working of that process (i.e. when the underlying mechanism is there with its activation conditions satisfied).

Understanding why a phenomenon occurs involves knowing what the characteristic results of a process are. Given this, it may seem paradoxical that there might be two types of situation in each of which the computer has exactly the same outputs given the same inputs and one has the same ignorance about the internal nature of both processes, yet in one of which one understands why 8 is output and in the other one does not. But it is not really paradoxical. In one situation one knows what are the characteristic results of a process that determines the output, and in the other one does not. This is despite the fact that one's structure of beliefs may be identical in the two situations.

Kim argues, as I do, for explanatory realism, the position that something is an explanation in virtue of the existence of some objective causal relation. But he thinks that this clearly 'leads to the propositional view of explanatory knowledge: it makes "having" an explanation a matter of knowing a certain proposition to be true' (Kim 1987, in Ruben 1993: 236). This is because Kim thinks that for an explanatory realist the knowledge required for understanding will simply be the knowledge that that causal relation holds. But, on my version of explanatory realism, the knowledge required for understanding is not just knowledge that a certain pair of events are causally related, but knowledge that a certain process happened. It is not clear that such knowledge will be best thought of as propositional.

The knowledge that is required involves knowledge of how the process resulting in the phenomenon works—what its characteristic stages are. In some cases this could be expressed as a fully specified proposition. But there is no guarantee that this is so. There might be no finite specification of how the process works that leaves absolutely no doubt about how the specification should be interpreted. And even if there is such a specification, a subject may not assent to it because of its great complexity (even though the subject may be able to assent to every basic condition of the specification taken individually).

In the industrial pursuit of Artificial Intelligence, computer scientists try to formulate logical specifications of how an expert does a certain task by painstakingly going through with the expert what they do in each type of situation. Assuming that it is possible to produce a correct specification, it should not be supposed that the expert knows that that specification is true. The expert might be surprised or sceptical that the specification could be abstracted from what they said. Yet there is no question that the expert knows how the task should be performed.

This suggests that knowledge of how a process works might be better thought of as possession of some intellectual capacity rather than as knowing some proposition. The capacity would be mastery of some way of describing the different results of the process in different circumstances. This is a more inclusive sort of knowledge than knowledge of a proposition specifying what the results of the process are in different circumstances. For, if one does know such a proposition, then, by the same token, one has mastery of a method of describing the results of the process in different circumstances. But, as in the case of the expert system, one might have mastery of such a method without knowing any such proposition.[12]

There is a further argument in favour of construing the knowledge involved in understanding as involving mastery of a method rather than as knowledge of a proposition. Suppose that a proposition could express what the characteristic results of a process resulting in some phenomenon were. In order to understand why the phenomenon occurred, does one need to *know* the proposition or just believe it? Suppose that all the information one has about the process, although true, was derived from an unreliable source, so that it is an accident that one's beliefs are true. Then one does not know the relevant proposition, but only believes it. Yet, I think that one understands the phenomenon just as well as someone who has the same beliefs but derived from a reliable source. One can know why the phenomenon occurs without knowing, rather than believing, the proposition about the process resulting in the phe-

---

[12] Paul Snowdon has persuaded me that the distinction between knowing-how and knowing-that cannot be so sharply drawn if one includes demonstrative identification in the propositional content of knowing-that. Knowing how to ride a bicycle might be construed as knowing that *this* is the way to ride a bicycle. One could not have this sort of knowledge unless 'this' had a reference and that requires actually being able to ride a bicycle. This is why I have made the contrast in the two kinds of knowledge that might be involved in understanding as the contrast between mastery of a method and knowledge of a *fully specified* proposition.

nomenon. So, what makes the state involved in understanding a state of knowledge is not that it involves knowing a proposition, but rather that it involves knowing how to do something. It involves mastery of a method. Consider as a parallel someone who learns how to speak French from a maniac who cannot speak French, but gives the right lessons by accident. If you place this person in France, it seems right to say that they understand French, and know how to speak French, even though they do not know any propositions about how French is spoken.

According to this account, then, in order to understand why a phenomenon occurs, one must have mastery of a method of deriving descriptions of the results of a process that results in the phenomenon, and one must see how the description of the phenomenon fits into this method. Roughly speaking, intelligibility is being identified with describability. A phenomenon is made intelligible by being incorporated in some theoretical method which gives one a way of describing that phenomenon. If that theoretical method represents the way the process works generally, then not only is the phenomenon intelligible but it is understood properly.

How does a theoretical method, T, describe how a causal process, P, works? In different types of circumstances P itself will have different results. We say that T represents P if and only if in all the different circumstances where P is happening, its results are those described by the results of T. In other words, how the process works is reflected by how the method works.

Many different things may count as methods of describing the results of a process. A law of Physics is one such method. By applying a law to different situations, one can derive different descriptions of what happens. For a law to work in this way, there is no need for it to be universally true. It must be true just to the extent that whenever the process it is supposed to represent is happening—the underlying mechanism is present and fully activated—then whatever the law describes as happening does happen. For a law to have a role in understanding, it need only be thought of as a method of inferring conclusions; there is no requirement that the inference involves deductive certainty.[13]

For example, consider the process of Newtonian gravitation. (I am assuming there is such a process.) Newton's Theory of Gravity

---

[13] This fits well with Cartwright's claims about laws (Cartwright 1983), and also reflects Ryle's conception of laws as 'inference-tickets' (Ryle 1949: 121).

provides descriptions of how things will interact which truly describe the results of the gravitational process. Whenever the Newtonian gravitation mechanism is working its results are what are described by the Newtonian Theory of Gravity.

This is not to say that in all circumstances the theory must determine descriptions that are true. For there is no need to consider those circumstances where the process is not happening. This is a consequence of the earlier claim that superficial knowledge of how a process works is all that is required for understanding why a phenomenon occurs. One does not need to have the underlying knowledge of the exact circumstances in which the process is happening. In strange Einsteinian situations Newton's Law of Gravity breaks down. These may be regarded as situations in which the Newtonian process of gravitation does not happen (and must be included in our notion of what the underlying mechanism is). This does not mean that Newton's theory is wrong. The worst we can say about it is that it does not embody universally true laws.

Understanding in Physics also involves the use of models and metaphors (see Hesse 1963). Again, these can just be thought of as ways of deriving descriptions of what should happen in different circumstances. As long as they correctly describe the way the actual process works by determining descriptions corresponding to the characteristic structure of stages of that process, then they are every bit as reputable as laws.

Historical understanding can be accounted for in the same sort of way. Generally, it involves being able to tell a story. Consider understanding why the Church of England was established as the key religious institution in England. This will consist in knowing a story describing Henry VIII's battle with Rome over his divorce, the dissolution of the monasteries, etc. We want to say that if the story is well understood there is something inevitable about the last part of it—about the establishment of the Church of England. This inevitability is certainly not logical necessity. It is the inevitability of the result of the correct application of a theoretical method.

If one has historical understanding of an event one must be able to use it to determine other descriptions than the one at issue, even if only the negation of the one at issue. 'If the pope had not been in league with Philip of Spain, then he would have been happy to annul Henry's marriage, and the Catholic Church would have remained in domination in England for some time.' Again note that we are not deriving conclusions from universally true laws. There is no need to rule out the logical possibility of some other cause for confrontation with Rome cropping up unexpectedly.

What the historical narrative does is to describe a process that resulted in the establishment of the Church of England. Implicit in the historical narrative is a theoretical method that determines descriptions of what should happen in different circumstances. In this situation it determines the description that the Church of England is established. This is what gives the conclusion its feeling of inevitability. In other circumstances other descriptions would be determined. The narrative is not just a series of facts about what happened; it also embodies a series of counterfactual conditionals that enable one to produce descriptions of what would have happened in other circumstances. One must be able to tell alternative stories.

A future-tense sentence may be determined by one method while it is contradicted by another. What it is *reasonable* to assert is determined by a wider consideration than just what description should be made according to one method. If a way of determining future descriptions determines the description that X will occur, we cannot thereby say that it is reasonable to assert that X will occur. However, we can say that a *conditional* assertion is rationally justified; i.e. 'According to this way of drawing descriptions, it *should* be the case that X occurs.' This is a kind of epistemological predetermination, however weak.

Having mastery of such a method does not in itself mean that one has antecedently applicable reasons for believing that the phenomenon would occur. If knowledge of interfering conditions is not necessary for such understanding, then one need not be in a knowledge position that would give one confidence antecedently that the phenomenon would occur. Certainly one does not need to have reason from which one could have *deduced* that the phenomenon would occur.

Moreover understanding why a phenomenon happens does not mean that one has the ability to identify the process antecedently. This means that one might lack even antecedent reason to believe that the phenomenon will happen if nothing goes wrong. For one's knowledge that a phenomenon is the result of a certain sort of process which underlies this sort of understanding is not something that one need have before the phenomenon occurs.

So being equipped with understanding of why a phenomenon occurs does not mean that one is equipped with anything that would have enabled one to conclude rationally that the phenomenon would occur in advance. What one is equipped with is something that enables one to determine in advance the *idea* that the phenomenon will occur. This only enables one to conclude that the phenomenon should occur according to that way of describing things.

This account captures some very small part of the flavour of Hempel's account of explanation. Hempel requires of someone who understands why a phenomenon occurs that they know an argument from which they can infer that that phenomenon occurs. A theoretical method of deriving descriptions is in a weak sense an argument. Where my account differs from Hempel's is that I do not require that such arguments be either deductively valid or inductively sound. I do not require that they provide good reasons for predicting in advance that the phenomenon should occur.

There may be worries now that such an epistemologically weak notion of intelligibility allows almost anything to be intelligible. If theoretical determination is not logical deduction, what is to stop it from being arbitrary and ridiculous? Must we impose constraints on what methods of forming descriptions may count as making things intelligible? I think not; for it is not the task of a theoretical method to make a necessarily right description. It is in the relation between the theoretical method and the real causal determination that the correctness or incorrectness of a way of describing the world is decided.

Consider a crazy theoretical method that incorporates the rule, 'Whenever someone walks under a ladder determine the description that ill luck will befall them.' This is at least a method of forming descriptions (as is indicated by the fact that people actually use it). It should not be discarded as a way of making something intelligible. For, if there was a process represented by this sort of superstitious method then the method could be used to explain cases of ill luck. So it is the world that does the work and not the theoretical method in distinguishing crazy explanations from good ones.[14]

[14] My account of theoretical methods is very close to Dennett's talk of 'stances' (1987: ch. 2). It differs in as much as he thinks that the point of occupying a stance is to be able to predict the future; I think that prediction is incidental to the purpose of understanding.

D. EXPLANATION

The notion of understanding that I have been trying to elucidate is not a relativistic one. Whether or not someone has mastery of a theoretical method is an objective fact testable by seeing whether or not the descriptions they come up with are correct for that theoretical method. Whether or not they know how the phenomenon to be explained fits into that method is an equally objective matter, as is the question of whether or not that method correctly describes a process which results in the phenomenon. Along with this notion of understanding is a correlative notion of explanation. Such an explanation is a way of providing that sort of understanding; it yields superficial knowledge of why the phenomenon occurred. So it provides mastery of a method of describing results which are the results of a process resulting in the phenomenon; and it provides a way of seeing how the phenomenon fits into that method.

There does not seem to be much prospect of finding a canonical way of providing such understanding. If the knowledge required for understanding is practical rather than propositional, then there is no guarantee that there is a fully specified proposition or set of such propositions which constitutes a correct explanation. Explanation is not just a question of providing facts, but it is also a question of teaching a technique. Not only is there no canonical way to teach a technique, but there are not even any objective criteria for what counts as an appropriate attempt at teaching a technique. Consider trying to make someone understand the kinetic theory of gases. Suppose you say to them: 'Think of a gas as a collection of billiard balls.' Whether this is a good move in teaching the theory depends on what conception the person has of a collection of billiard balls. Their conception might be conditioned by the thought that one purpose of billiards is to pot the balls, in which case, thinking of a gas as a collection of billiard balls may be unhelpful.

If this is right, then there are no objective criteria for what constitutes a *complete* explanation of why a phenomenon occurs; nor are there objective criteria for what constitutes part of a complete explanation of why a phenomenon occurs. This is a stronger conclusion than Lewis's (1986). He argues that there is no such thing as a complete explanation, since there is an indefinite amount of information about the causal history of a phenomenon, and all such information is part of the explanation of that phenomenon.

But he does have a simple objective criterion for what constitutes part of an explanation—namely that it must provide some information about the causal history. His account can have such a criterion because he presumes that all knowledge about the causal history of some phenomenon is propositional.

Lewis and, following him, Lipton (1990) suggest that if you want a tighter notion of what constitutes part of an explanation of a phenomenon the explanandum can be expanded to include a contrast class for that phenomenon. As Lipton points out, the Big Bang is part of the causal history of every single event, but is not explanatory of very many of them. If a contrast class is provided along with the explanandum, then the relevant part of the causal history can be narrowed down dramatically. The Big Bang is not part of the explanation of why 8 rather than 15 was output by the computer program considered earlier, since had 15 been output, the Big Bang would have been part of the causal history of that event too. Only those events which were part of the causal history of 8 being output, but would not have been part of the causal history of 15 being output, are part of the contrastive explanation.

According to my account, including a contrast class with the explanandum, although it will narrow down what constitutes a part of an explanation, will not enable one to devise objective criteria for what constitutes part of an explanation. If you want to know why 8 rather than 15 was output by the computer, then either you have some misleading beliefs that suggest that 15 should be output—perhaps you think that the computer was multiplying its inputs or that the inputs were, say, 10 and 5 rather than 3 and 5—or you have enough understanding to know why 8 or 15 should be output, but not enough to know why 8 should be. So, there are two kinds of explanation that will give you understanding in such cases. (*a*) You may be told what sort of process it is which is happening; for example, it is an addition rather than a multiplication process. (*b*) You may be told what sort of circumstances were in place; for example, the inputs were 3 and 5 rather than 10 and 5.

Asking a contrastive question, for example why 8 rather than 15 was output, is a way of narrowing down what constitutes part of an explanation. But it does not ensure that there will be objective criteria for what counts as part of an explanation. This is so, because if you need to know what sort of process it is which results in the thing to be explained, then you may need to be taught how it works, and, as I have argued, there may be no objective criterion for what counts as part of such a lesson.

Given this, the way to ensure that one has an objective criterion for what counts as part of an explanation is to ignore that part of an explanation which concerns what kind of process is operating. Instead, one should limit one's attention to that part of understanding which involves knowing how the phenomenon fits into the characteristic structure of stages of the process resulting in it. The point is that this latter type of knowledge, unlike the former, is propositional. For example, if we can assume knowledge that an addition process is happening, we can explain why 8 was output from the computer by saying that 3 and 5 were input.

A very narrow and rather technical notion of a reason can be extracted from this discussion. In the computer example, that 3 and 5 were the inputs counts as a reason that 8 was output, in virtue of the fact that there is a theoretical method representing a process resulting in 8 being output which would not determine the description that 8 should be output if the reason were not available to that theoretical method. The way a process works which results in 8 being output is sensitive to whether it is the case that 3 and 5 are input. Let me call such a reason a *circumstantial reason*. So, here is my general definition of a circumstantial reason:

> Phenomenon, *P*, occurs because of circumstantial reason, *R*, if and only if there is a theoretical method, *T*, that determines a description of *P* and represents the characteristic stages of a process that results in *P* itself; and *T* would not determine a description of *P* if *R* were not available to it.

The point of giving a definition of such a restricted notion of a reason is to meet Achinstein's challenge to find a non-relativistic notion of explanation. I do not mean to deny that explaining how the process resulting in the phenomenon works is a part of explanation, understood more generally, nor that descriptions belonging to such explanation would normally be called 'reasons'. For example, a law of nature would normally count as a reason even though it is *part* of a theoretical method rather than a fact which is available to the method.

Despite being very narrow, this notion of a circumstantial reason will turn out to be rich enough to be at the heart of the account of teleological explanation given in the next chapter. The only task remaining in this chapter is to go back to the two arguments given in Chapter 1—the Argument from False Beliefs and the Argument from the Impotence of Unrepresented Facts. I claimed then that they were both based on false premisses about the nature of explanation.

In the case of the Argument from the Impotence of Unrepresented Facts, the relevant assumption was that a complete set of reasons for some phenomenon should form a logically sufficient set for that phenomenon. Given my account of explanation, this is clearly an unwarranted assumption. Even if the complete set of reasons included a complete description of how the process works in addition to all the circumstantial reasons, it need not be possible to deduce the fact that the phenomenon will occur. This is because the process which is being described is not always happening. It only happens when its underlying conditions are realized, and the satisfaction of these conditions is not part of the explanation of why the phenomenon happened, but is instead part of the explanation of why the process resulting in the phenomenon was happening.

In the case of the Argument from False Beliefs, the relevant assumption was the following:

P3. If phenomenon *P* can be completely explained without reference to *X*, then *X* is not an essential part of any immediate explanation of *P*.

The thought behind this assumption is that there is something wrong with explanatory overdetermination. There cannot be distinct explanations working with distinct sets of circumstantial reasons both accounting for the same thing. If a phenomenon has been accounted for then it cannot be accounted for again.

To assess this thought, it is important to distinguish different kinds of overdetermination. First, there is the purely theoretical kind of overdetermination. An example of this is the case of the story of Jones being poisoned by arsenic and the story of Jones being run over by a bus both determining the description that Jones will die. In this case, only the process of being run over by a bus causally determines the actual event of her dying. Since the poisoning does not explain her death, there is no explanatory overdetermination.

Next there is causal overdetermination by processes of sorts which one would usually think of as competing for causal influence since they are described at the same level of description. An example of this might be the case of two bullets piercing someone's heart simultaneously. Is it right to describe this as a case of two separate processes individually resulting in someone's death, with two quite distinct sets of circumstantial reasons? Many people would think not (see e.g. Kim 1987). It is argued that if there really is no way of separating out one of the processes as the one that resulted in the death, then what resulted in the death must be a conglomerate process involving both bullets. There is no way of describing the situation which keeps separate two processes involving the death. This is because the death would have to be part of both processes, and since we are assuming that the processes are described at the same level of description, there is no level of description at which one can draw a line around a process involving the death and just one of the bullets. If this argument is correct, such an example is not in fact a case of causal overdetermination and poses no threat to P3.

There is a third type of explanatory overdetermination, however, which is much more threatening to P3. This is where there are two or more distinct but metaphysically interdependent processes which are not described at the same level of description and which result in the same phenomenon. It is not clear that the argument against the possibility of overdetermination of someone's death by two shooting processes applies here. For, if just one of the processes resulting in the phenomenon is described, then, at some level of description, a complete story has been given; and similarly for the other process(es).

3

Teleological Explanation

A. ARISTOTLE'S CONCEPTION OF TELEOLOGICAL EXPLANATION

Aristotle defines teleological explanation as explanation of something in terms of what that thing is for the sake of.

Again, in the sense of end or that for the sake of which a thing is done, e.g. walking about is done for the sake of health. ('Why is he walking about?' We say: 'To be healthy', and having said that, we think we have assigned the cause.) (*The Physics* 194ᵇ32–35.)

If walking is good for health, and my walking can be explained by that reason, then it is teleologically explained. If a flower is for the sake of attracting insects and that is why a plant has one, then the presence of the flower is teleologically explained. If my going to the bank is for the sake of getting out some money, and that explains why I go to the bank, then that action is teleologically explained.

What it is for something to be for the sake of something else is for it to be a means to the end of that thing—a way of achieving that thing. Saying that something is a means to an end of something is a way of justifying it, at least in the weak sense that I introduced in Chapter 1. I do not mean that something is justified in any final way in virtue of being a means to an end. If the end is bad, then the means to that end is not ultimately justified by it. Even if the end is itself justified, the means to that end is not always ultimately justified by it, since it may be wrong for other reasons. My claim is just that saying that something is a means to an end is a *way* of justifying it, even if it is not always a very good way.

It is an interesting question whether all practical justifications involve means-end justifications. If they do not, then there is a discrepancy between teleological explanation as I am defining it here and teleological explanation as I defined it in Chapter 1. There,

I said that teleological explanation was explanation in terms of practical justification. Here I am saying that teleological explanation is explanation in terms of means-end justification. If there is a discrepancy here, it would mean that the characterization of the Teleological Theory of Action would have to be altered slightly. I shall return to the question of the nature of practical justification in the next chapter.

Aristotle's notion of 'for the sake of' did not distinguish between cases of actions being for the sake of achieving goals and cases of natural features being for the sake of serving functions. He wrote (196^b22): 'Things that are for the sake of something include whatever may be done as a result of thought or of nature.'

Somebody's walking about is teleologically explained if it is explained in terms of the fact that walking is for the sake of health. Similarly, the presence of one's teeth is teleologically explained if it is explained in terms of the fact that teeth are for the sake of eating (198^b25 ff.). However, standard modern approaches to teleological explanation divide into two quite separate treatments: one of the teleological explanation of action and the other of the teleological explanation of the products of nature.

A typical internalist formulation of a teleological explanation of action is 'X happened because the agent intended X to happen'. This is often articulated into 'X happened because the agent intended G to happen and believed that X would bring about G'. A typical formulation of teleological explanation in nature is 'X happened because X tends to bring about G'.

On the face of it, there is a major division between these forms of explanation. In particular, one depends on mental states while the other does not. Woodfield (1976: 205–18) argues that they both count as teleological only because of a grammatical similarity. This is the similarity between 'X happened because X leads to G and G is good' and 'X happened because it was believed that X leads to G and G is good'. He thinks that 'the essence of teleology lies in welding a causal element and an evaluative element to yield an explanatory device' (1976: 216). However, 'when Aristotle said that it didn't matter whether a teleological end was actually good or apparently good, he encouraged the conflation of two quite different conceptions of what an end is' (1976: 211). According to Woodfield, although the difference between 'good' and 'apparently good' is minor on the superficial linguistic level, it leads to a radical difference in one's account of teleological explanation.

Against Woodfield's argument I would like to make this claim: it is only to the extent that the reasons given in putative teleological explanations constitute practical justifications of what they aim to explain that such explanations count as teleological. And the fact that both sorts of explanation are explanations in terms of practical justification confers a deep level of unity on them.

Take explanation of action first. As many people (including Davidson 1980: essay 1) have pointed out, when we ask for a reason for an action, we are asking for a justification as well as for a cause. It is only in as much as an agent's belief that X leads to G and desire to achieve G constitute a practical reason or justification for doing X that explaining an action in terms of them constitutes explaining the action in terms of what it is for the sake of. If a structure of intentional mental states failed to justify an action at all, then explanation of the action in terms of it would not be teleological.

The same goes for externalist explanations in nature. It is only in as much as the fact that X leads to G constitutes some sort of practical justification of X that it can be a teleological reason for X happening. The teleological question 'Why do we have teeth?' is asking for a justification of teeth as well as a cause of them. Implicit in the question is the question 'Why should we have teeth?' The fact that possession of teeth leads to the animal being able to eat fills both roles; and it is only in virtue of this that it may be a teleological reason.

There is some debate as to whether Aristotle regarded teleological explanation as a kind of causal explanation. We might translate *The Physics* 194^{b}30–36 as follows:

'Why is he walking about?' We say: 'To be healthy', and having said that, we have assigned the cause. The same is true of the intermediate steps which we brought about through the action of something else as means towards the end.

But this passage is open to the obvious counter-interpretation that Aristotle means by 'cause' just 'reason'. A 'formal cause' is a special kind of explanation rather than a special kind of causation. So why should we not say the same about final causes (see Annas 1982)? However, it is becoming more usual nowadays to interpret Aristotle as regarding teleological explanation as a species of causal explanation after all (see Cooper 1987 and Gotthelf 1987).

I think that it should be accepted that teleological explanation is supposed to be a kind of causal explanation in as much as it is supposed to say something informative about the causal process resulting in the thing to be explained. Although a teleological explanation does not cite some preceding event which brought about the result (and is thus distinguished from other sorts of causal explanation), it does purport to say something about how the result came about. When one says that some event, X, happened because it was for the sake of some goal, G, the truth of this depends on the nature of the process causally resulting in X; that X was for the sake of G must be relevant somehow to the working of that causal process.

There may be a worry that if teleological explanation is a kind of causal explanation, then this means that causation can go backwards in time. If a phenomenon is causally explained in a way that is represented by means-ends justification, then it may be causally explained in terms of the achievement of a later goal. Does this not mean that the achievement of the later goal causally influences the phenomenon?

The internalist response is that all that is required for teleological explanation is that a *representation* of the goal explains the phenomenon. This response is immune to the backwards causation problem. But for an externalist, no such response is possible. If we allow that some activity occurs because it is a means to the achievement of a *particular* future end state, and we assume this to be a causal explanation, then we must conclude that the future state causally influences the prior activity. But this implication can be avoided by realizing that teleological activity is explained with respect to a *general* type of future state rather than a particular token of a future state. So we can say that some teleological activity occurs because it is a means to a certain type of future state without in any way implicating backwards causation.

Someone who still thinks that there is a problem here with backwards causation may have the mistaken thought that a real causal process cannot be represented by a theoretical method that goes off into future descriptions before coming back to describing the result. Such a process would seem to have to go forwards then backwards; but processes only go forwards. The thought is mistaken because there is no reason to suppose that the stages of the teleological process must work in the same order as the stages of the theoretical method which determines descriptions of the results of the process.

It might be thought that there is a problem with the idea that in different circumstances that part of the application of the theoretical method that results in the description of the means given the description of the end could be altered. The description of the future end state would remain unaltered while the description of the means to that end alters. If the actual teleological process is represented by this, then the result must be altered by circumstances that affect how that result leads to the end it is a means to. This looks like backwards causation again.

But of course it is not backwards causation. For this is exactly the way teleological processes do work. If something blocks the causal path from turning the tap to satisfying one's thirst (e.g. the water supply is cut off), then some other result like buying some bottled water will occur while the future state remains unaltered. All that is required to avoid backwards causation is that the circumstances that affect how the result leads to the future state should have come into being before the result is determined. Since the theoretical method only has access to information about how the world is before the result occurs, this is ensured.

Aristotle's conception of teleological explanation has come under pressure from the spirit of scientific unification in the last few hundred years. The science of Physics is supposed to work exclusively with non-teleological causal explanation. All other science is supposed to take Physics as a paradigm; and if an explanation is not scientific, it is taken to be worthless. So, if teleological explanation cannot be reduced somehow to non-teleological explanation, it is not a valid form of explanation at all.

Appeal to teleology is regarded by many as an appeal to magic. This is because such an appeal attributes values with a causal power in nature. Teleological explanation is causal explanation in terms of a practical justification. If there is anything in nature which can be explained teleologically, then whether or not such a thing is justified causally influences whether or not it happens. It happens because it should happen. It is a very comforting thought that nature is sensitive to what should happen, but most people think that now we must reject that thought utterly. Going against the tide of this rejection, I want to revive the thought, and argue that there are things in nature—namely actions—which do happen because they should.

B. DEVIANT CAUSAL CHAINS

What makes teleological explanation a special sort of explanation, distinct from the standard patterns of explanation found in Physics, is not just the special teleological nature of the reasons that figure in the explanation. It is also that the whole process being described by the explanation is teleological. This can be seen by the possibility of non-teleological reasons being part of teleological explanations and by the possibility of teleological reasons being part of non-teleological explanations.

An explanation of something in terms of a means-end explanation may include various circumstantial reasons that do not mention goals. Consider giving, as one reason for my going to the bank, that I had run out of money. This reason makes no reference to any goals; it does not cite an end as an explanation of a means. It may or may not fit into a practical justification of my going to the bank.

On the one hand, one of my goals may be having enough money, and going to the bank may be a means to the end of having enough money if I have run out. There is then a system of practical justification which yields the description that I should go to the bank when I have run out of money. If the process resulting in my behaviour works according to this system, then my behaviour is teleologically explained, and that I had run out of money is a circumstantial reason in this teleological explanation.

On the other hand, I may be living in a world in which banks have no money, they just have bank clerks. Suppose that I went to the cashpoint machine, which we assume is not inside the bank, in order to get some money. Suppose that the machine swallowed up my card after giving me my money, and I went to the bank to complain to the manager. In this case, there is a teleological explanation of my going to the cashpoint machine, in which my running out of money is a circumstantial reason. There is also a teleological explanation of my going to the bank, in which the machine swallowing my card is a circumstantial reason. But there is no teleological explanation of my going to the bank, in which my running out of money is a circumstantial reason. The explanation, in which that

figures as a circumstantial reason, represents two teleological processes and a cashpoint-machine-breaking-down process. It is not
itself a teleological process. That the machine has broken down is
not an input to that process, since it happens during the course of
that process. So, going to the bank is not practically justified by the
inputs to the process.

This example raises the possibility of teleological reasons figuring
in non-teleological explanations. The more familiar manifestation
of this in the philosophy of action is the possibility of deviant (or
wayward) causal chains. This is particularly familiar in the context
of internalist teleological explanations of behaviour.[1] Here is
Davidson's famous example (1980: 79):

A climber might want to rid himself of the weight and danger of holding
another man on a rope, and he might know that by loosening his hold on
the rope he could rid himself of the weight and danger. This belief and
want might so unnerve him as to cause him to loosen his hold, and yet it
might be the case that he never *chose* to loosen his hold, nor did he do it
intentionally.

In this example, the belief and want, which are supposed to practically justify the climber's activity, also cause it. But they cause it in
a way that makes it accidental that practically justified activity
occurs. Although a practical justification of the activity explains the
occurrence of the activity, it does not do so in such a way that we
would want to describe the activity as teleologically explained.
There is a teleological circumstantial reason in the explanation, but
that is not enough to make the explanation itself teleological. The
loosening of the climber's hold does not occur for the sake of
dropping the other man.

It is not so commonly realized that the possibility of deviant
causal chains is a problem for externalist teleological explanation
just as much as it is for internalist teleological explanation. For
example, Larry Wright's influential account is open to counter-
examples involving deviant chains. He writes (1976: 39):

S does B for the sake of G iff:
   (i) B tends to bring about G.
   (ii) B occurs because (i.e., is brought about by the fact that) it tends to
       bring about G.

---

[1] See Chisholm (1966: 29–30), Davidson (1980: 78–9), Goldman (1970: 62). A
good treatment of some of the more modern material on deviant causal chains in
action is Moya (1990: ch. 11).

This account is broadly Aristotelian. That B tends to bring about G can be seen as a way of expressing the requirement that B is a means to the end of achieving G. (I will discuss whether it expresses this requirement successfully in the next chapter.) Given this, Wright is claiming that something is teleologically explained if it is explained in terms of a means-end justification for it. He adapts this to give an account of functions, by saying roughly that something has Z as its function if it is there for the sake of achieving Z. So (1976: 81):

The function of X is Z iff:
    (i) Z is a consequence (result) of X's being there,
    (ii) X is there because it does (results in) Z.

Wright gives his account of teleological explanation in terms of teleological circumstantial reasons, and so is vulnerable to examples where there is a circumstantial reason which is teleological though the process as a whole is not. Consider this example. Suppose that a species of deer is subject to an occasional genetic mutation resulting in an extra long nose. Having this extra length has two consequences for a deer. It enables it to smell tigers better, and it results in uncontrollable sneezing from time to time. Its main predator is a kind of tiger on the brink of extinction. The only remaining female tiger is on the point of dying of starvation when she hears a mutant deer sneezing, and goes and eats it. This enables the tigers to survive this low point and go on to thrive. The deer without the long noses all get eaten because they cannot smell their predators, and the long nose becomes a feature of the species.

Now, according to this story, the long nose is a feature of the later deer population partly because having a long nose results in the deer sneezing, and this in turn results in the deer being noticed by a hungry tiger in the vicinity. So Wright's conditions are satisfied. There is a teleological circumstantial reason, namely that having a long nose is a means to the end of sneezing and so of attracting and feeding tigers. But it is not a teleological explanation. It is no part of the function of the long nose that it results in sneezing, nor that it results in attracting tigers and getting its owner eaten. The problem is that the fact that having a long nose is a means to the end of attracting tigers and getting eaten causally explains the selection of long noses as a feature of the species in the *wrong sort of way*. The *process* resulting in the presence of long noses is not sensitive to whether or not having a long nose is a means to sneezing. If some other feature, like having long whiskers, was a means to sneezing, this feature would not result from the process.

My diagnosis of deviant causal chain examples is that they represent situations where the right sort of cause occurs but the wrong sort of process happens. Equivalently, the right sort of circumstantial reason holds, but the wrong sort of theoretical explanatory method describes the process. This is the same sort of diagnosis that Davidson among many others provides when he says that the 'point is that not just any causal connection between rationalizing attitudes and a wanted effect suffices to guarantee that producing the wanted effect was intentional. The causal chain must follow the right sort of route' (Davidson 1980: 79).

Davidson despaired of spelling out 'a way in which attitudes must cause actions if they are to rationalize the action' (1980: 79). As Moya says (1990: 118), reflecting Davidson's own tentative suggestion, a 'natural move to be made is to suggest that the causal chain must operate in such a way that it corresponds, at least roughly, to the pattern of the subject's practical reasoning'. Unfortunately, keeping hold of the notion of a causal chain, rather than of a causal process, in one's account dooms it to failure. This is because we can always invent examples of deviant causal chains by interpolating between any two stages of the chain some deviant chain.

For example, a good suggestion by Brand and others is to require of intentional action that the agent follow a plan (see Brand 1984: 23–30). But, if a plan is conceived of as a causal chain, it cannot be conceived of as an infinitely detailed chain. So, however detailed it is, there is always room to interpolate some deviance into the chain while the plan remains the same. In fact, following a plan should not be thought of as a causal chain, but rather as a process. This claim depends crucially on my account of processes in the previous chapter which distinguishes a process from a causal chain. Interpolating some deviance into a process does change the process as I shall show shortly. So, unless one's account of following a plan includes an account of processes, it will not be much good.

As Brand notes, not all cases of deviance can be attributed to failure to follow a plan. The example of the climber from Davidson cannot be treated this way, since there is no plan usually involved in loosening one's grip. Brand's diagnosis in such cases is that 'there is causal space, as it were, between the mental antecedent and the beginning of the causal chain leading to the overt behaviour' (1984: 19). His cure is to not allow any such causal space, and require of the causal chain that the link between the mental antecedent and the start of the overt behaviour be proximate.

In my view, Dennett (1991) quite successfully debunks the picture of the mind according to which there is some point in the causal neurophysiological chain from afferent nerve impulses to efferent nerve impulses where the mental suddenly stops. Brand's solution to the problem of deviant causal chains depends on this picture. It also depends on a theory of causation according to which there are such things as proximate causal events. And, even if his solution made sense, it would only rule out the possibility of deviant causal chains at one precise point in the causal chain somewhere deep in the brain. There is still plenty of scope to interpolate deviant causal chains within the non-mental chain leading up to the overt behaviour.

It is time to spell out my solution in some detail. The main idea is that for something to be teleologically explained it is not sufficient that there be a teleological circumstantial reason; the theoretical method underpinning the explanation must be teleological. It is not enough that there is a teleological cause; the whole process must be teleological. This means that the characteristic results of a process resulting in the phenomenon must be describable by a method of means-end justification.

According to my account of what a causal process is, this is a stronger requirement than that there should be a causal chain whose stages accord with some structure of means-end justification. Rather, there must be some underlying nature present which is responsible for results happening in accordance with a means-end justification, whatever that happens to be in the circumstances. This underlying nature must be such that if something else accorded with means-end justification, it would result instead. So a wider set of counterfactual conditionals must be supported than would be supported by a simple causal chain from reason to activity. It is not just that if that reason had not held then that activity would not have happened. But it is also that if some other reason had held, then activity corresponding to that other reason would have happened.

Consider Davidson's climber and contrast him with a climber in the same situation who *does* loosen his grip intentionally. In both cases the loosening of the grip is the result of a process in which the relevant belief and desire form a circumstantial reason. But the processes in each case are quite different. The process resulting in the intentional action works in a way which is sensitive to what is required to achieve a means to an end. The process resulting in the nervous twitch does not. Although the way this process works is sensitive to whether or not the belief–desire pair is present, it does not have the broader sensitivity to whatever has a means-end justification in the circumstances. If it was clear that what was required in order to drop the other climber was a tightening of the wrist, this would not result from the process. The grip would still loosen even if it was not appropriate. In the case of intentional action, it is not accidental that activity according to a means-end justification happens. In the case of the nervous twitch, it is accidental. This is because in the case of the intentional action a process results in the activity, which, whenever it happens, will always result in practically justified activity. Whereas, in the case of the nervous twitch, no such process results in the activity. Perhaps, such a process would have resulted in the activity, but the process of nervously twitching got in there first.

You cannot interpolate a deviant causal chain into the stages of a teleological *process* and still have the same teleological *process* happening. This is because the process with a deviant causal chain will have different characteristic stages. Even if it results in the same thing on this occasion, the presence of the deviant chain will mean that there will be some situations in which the augmented process is happening where it does not result in what it should according to the means-end justification. This is by contrast with teleological *causal chains*. You can always interpolate a deviant causal chain into a teleological causal chain and still have the same teleological causal chain. This is why the problem of deviant causal chains can only be solved with an account of processes as distinct from causal chains.

It is always possible to interpolate strange causal loops into teleological processes without changing the characteristic stages of the process. For example, you could interpolate a radio signal going to a satellite and back in the causal pathway of a nerve impulse being sent down the arm. If the overall process had exactly the same set of characteristic results as the original process, then it would be a teleological process of exactly the same type as the original. In such cases we have no problem with describing the resultant activity as teleologically explained and hence as intentional. The extra loop does not make the causal chain deviant since it makes no difference to the way the process works.

The same analysis works for the problem of deviant causal chains in externalist teleological explanation. In my example of the deer, the process that results in long noses becoming a feature of the deer population does not result generally in whatever is a means to the end of getting the deer noticed by tigers. If something different had been required, like having a pungent odour, for example, this would not have resulted from the process. On the other hand, if there are genuinely teleological processes in nature, then they will have just this sort of sensitivity. For example, the process that results in white colouration in moths that settle on a particular kind of tree *would* result in black colouration if that was a means to the end of being camouflaged against such trees.[2]

Thalberg has a proposal to avoid deviant causal chains in the explanation of action which gets pretty close to talking about processes. He describes standard cases of deviance as follows (1984: 257):

> The person's intention only inaugurates a sequence of causally related goings-on which terminate in behaviour; it does not *continue* to shape events, particularly the behaviour. I think a full-blown causal theory prescribes a tighter hookup—what I call 'ongoing,' 'continuous' or 'sustained' causation.

I think that what Thalberg is after here is a notion of a teleological *process*. But, because his notion of sustained causation does not quite get there, his proposal is open to the following counter-example from Moya (1990: 121–2). A man, intending to run over his uncle in the street, finds his path blocked by an old pedestrian in the middle of the road. He drives through him in order not to miss the chance to run down his uncle. But, of course, the old pedestrian is his uncle. All his behaviour was sustained by his

---

[2] I consider whether evolution really is teleological in the next section. My claim here is just that if evolution is a teleological process, then my way of eliminating the problem of deviant causal chains will work here just as well as it does for action.

intentions and beliefs; nevertheless, he did not intentionally run down his uncle.

Thalberg claims to have helped us understand Adam Morton's tantalizingly brief discussion of responsiveness with his own treatment of sustained causation. But I think that Morton's suggestion that 'intentional action is action that is guided by information to which it is responsive' (1975: 14) gets closer to the mark, though it needs a lot of working out. In some sense, the uncle-killer's behaviour was not responsive to information concerning what was a means to the end of running down his uncle. For, if there had been room to pass by the old pedestrian rather than driving through him, then the uncle-killer would have done that. If his behaviour had been properly responsive, he should not have done so.

Christopher Peacocke too accepts the vague suggestion 'that intentional behaviour is in some way characteristically sensitive to certain facts' (1979: 57). His own way of spelling out the details of this suggestion is quite complex. But, as I do, he thinks that giving an account of explanation is part of it. The key notion for Peacocke is that of differential explanation, which he defines as follows (1979: 66):

x's being ϕ differentially explains y's being ψ iff x's being ϕ is a non-redundant part of the explanation of y's being ψ, and according to the principles of explanation (laws) invoked in this explanation, there are functions . . . specified in these laws such that y's being ψ is fixed by these functions from x's being ϕ.

As far as I can see this coincides with my conception of explanation. Peacocke's 'differential explanation' is just normal causal explanation in my account. As such it does not rule out the possibility of deviant causal chains, since in such cases it is still right to say that the attitudes explain the activity. The point is that the 'principles of explanation (laws) invoked in this explanation' are not the appropriate ones; they are not teleological. But Peacocke, while recognizing that these principles must be constrained in order to rule out deviant causal chains, instead of making this obvious move, introduces the constraint of 'stepwise recoverability' (1979: 79–84).

This is the constraint that at each stage of the causal chain one can work out what must have been present at the previous stage. This works against Davidson's example of the climber, since at the stage in the causal process where the nervousness appears, one might know enough to know that the climber's grip would be loosened without being able to recover any knowledge of the original attitude that caused the nervousness. But, unfortunately for Peacocke's account, it is easy enough to think of examples of deviant causal chains which satisfy this constraint. For example, suppose that after an accident there is not enough strength in my fingers to do very much with them, though my companion can see by faint movements what I intend to do. If she is feeling charitable to me, she may decide to move my fingers for me in the way that she sees I intend to move them. The movements of my fingers are not teleologically explained in terms of my attitudes alone; they are not my actions. Yet, at every stage of the causal process resulting in the movements, knowledge of what was happening at the previous stage can be recovered. Ultimately, knowledge of my intentions can be recovered from knowledge of my fingers' movements.

So, stepwise recoverability is not the right constraint to rule out deviant causal chains. The right constraint is that the theoretical method—the 'principles of explanation'—underlying the explanation—should be a method of means-end practical justification. Then the process described by that method will be a teleological process. Charles Taylor gets it almost exactly right (1964: 9):

> To offer a teleological explanation of some event or class of events, e.g., the behaviour of some being, is, then, to account for it by laws in terms of which an event's occurring is held to be dependent on that event's being required for some end. To say that the behaviour of a given system should be explained in terms of purpose, then, is, in part, to make an assertion about the form of laws, or the type of laws which hold of the system.

It may be a bit optimistic of Taylor to assume that a scheme of means-end justification can be expressed in a set of laws saying that an event will occur if it is required for some end. I return to this in the next section. But apart from this, he has provided a simple account of teleological explanation, which, in my view, is completely right and also immune from deviant causal chain counter-examples. The behaviour of the system which is Davidson's climber is not governed by principles of explanation (laws) in which an event's occurring is held to be dependent on that event being required for some end or on any other scheme of means-end justification.

Larry Wright's account (quoted earlier), which aims to be an improvement on Taylor's, in this respect at least, is much worse. He does not like Taylor's condition that the event being explained must be *required* for some end. And I think he is right in this. But he also leaves out of his own account any mention of the laws or principles of explanation governing the behaviour of the system whose behaviour is being explained. Thus he leaves his account open to counter-examples of deviant causal chains. I take it that Boorse's example of the leak in the chlorine pipe (Boorse 1976) and other similar examples involve deviant causal chains in my sense.

One advantage of Peacocke's account of deviant causal chains is that it is generalizable to all the areas of philosophy where the problem arises. In fact, the problem arises in every single area where there is a causal theory. There are deviant causal chain objections to the causal theories of perception, knowledge, and reference as well as to the teleological causal theories of function, purpose, and action. It is a very attractive strategy, if it works, to consign the problem of deviant causal chains to the philosophy of explanation rather than to regard it as a separate problem in the philosophy of mind, the philosophy of action, epistemology, the philosophy of science, and the philosophy of language. My account is generalizable in just the way Peacocke's is. The general strategy in each of these areas is to deny that we are looking for a requirement on the kind of cause involved, but to say instead that we are looking for a requirement on the kind of causal process involved.

C. THE MEANS-END RELATION

What sorts of things are means and ends, and how do they relate to each other? There are several closely related concepts to that of a means: a route; a method; a set of instructions or directions; a plan; a recipe. None of these is of much help for me in explicating the notion of a means, since they all appear to presuppose the notion of action. Although, in the end, the notion of means and of action are to be closely tied together, this is not a connection I want to introduce yet, since, in Chapter 5, I want to use the notion of a means to explicate that of action.

A more fundamental place to start is with the notion of an

answer to a how-question. How-questions can be asked of actions, and the answers describe means. For example:

How do you get to Brighton from here?
How do you make a Waldorf Salad?
How did she make herself into a millionaire?
How did he assassinate the president?

But how-questions can also be asked of things which are not actions. For example:

How did this stone get so hot?
How does a tree transplant nutrients?
How do supernovae come about?

To each of these questions, the answer describes a *way*: the way this stone got so hot; the way a tree transports nutrients; the way supernovae come about. Similarly with the first set of questions: the way to get to Brighton from here; etc.

As with why-questions, the adequacy of answers to how-questions depends on pragmatic factors. Different background information may be taken for granted by the answer and different levels of detail may be gone into. For example, the way this stone got so hot was by being exposed to direct midday sunshine for a couple of hours. Or, the way this stone got so hot was by absorbing more heat from the electromagnetic radiation from the sun than it transmitted back to the air over a period of two hours. Or, the way this stone got so hot was by the combined processes of the sun's thermonuclear reactions resulting in emission of radiation, which then travelled relatively unimpeded from the sun to the earth; it passed through the earth's atmosphere losing only X per cent of its energy; Y coulombs of this energy hit the stone and Z per cent of it was absorbed by the surface molecules, increasing their agitation; and so on.

What each of these answers has in common is that it describes a structure of processes and events which eventually results in the stone being very hot. Each part of the structure contributes to the whole by its results enabling later processes or events in the structure to occur or influencing the outcome of later processes or events or by themselves constituting the achievement of the required end. (From now on, I will use the word 'activity' to stand for either processes or events.)

So a way is a causally integrated structure of activity which eventually leads to the state of affairs which is the end of the way. More or less detailed ways can be specified in any particular case. Each will be a different carving up of what happens leading up to the result in question. Given what I have said about the identity of processes in Chapter 2, Section B, I do not think that these different structures will be reducible to one another even though what underlies each of them is the same. A complete account might have to spell out what constraints, if any, should operate over the notion of a causally integrated structure of activity, but I will not attempt to do that here. It is worth remarking that a way corresponds to what the Russellian account described in Chapter 2, Section B, would call a process, though, since a way has temporal (possibly overlapping) parts, I would call it an event.

This notion of a way corresponds roughly with Brand's notion of an action plan (1984: 27). 'P is an action plan for Aing *iff* P is a tree structure from (A1, A2, . . . A_n), where n $\geqslant$ 1 and where each A_{i+1} is dependent on A_i.' Obviously, a lot more work could be done on spelling out this notion of a way or a plan. But I only need to assume that something like this works.

I suggest that the notion of a means to an end can be understood in terms of that of a way. A means to an end is a sub-series of a way to the end being realized. (When we talk of *the* means rather than of *a* means to an end, we usually mean the whole of the way rather than just part of it; but nothing much rests on this distinction.)

However, it seems that not just any way counts as a means. Although the process of the sun warming the stone is the way the stone gets hot, it is absurd to say that this is a *means* to the stone becoming hot. It seems that a means must be somehow controllable; it must potentially be an action. However, if this is included as a constraint on what counts as a means, my project of providing an account of action in terms of means-end justification is threatened. If part of what it was for something to be a means was that it was potentially an action, then the account would involve circularity. The circularity would not make the account completely useless; we would still have an account of what makes something an actual action in terms of its being a potential action. However, the objection of circularity would fall away altogether if an account of what a means is could be provided which made no use of the notion of action.

To understand the notion of means we have to move from considering actual ways of some result happening to considering hypothetical ways of that result happening. A description of a hypothetical way can include descriptions of bits of activity which do not occur but which are in some sense available. The notion of availability should be thought of as an analogue to the notion of controllability, but with no presumption of agency. The availability of some piece of activity is relative to a basic repertoire of available activity.[3] It can be defined inductively as follows.

> Activity is available if and only if:
> either   (i) it is in the repertoire of basic activity
> or   (ii) it has a way consisting only of a structure of available activity along with other bits of activity which would happen if the rest of the structure happened.

A means is just defined as an available piece of activity. For example, suppose that we have a robot and we count certain movements of the robot's arm as in the repertoire of basic available activity. Suppose also that the robot is positioned with a welding torch in its hand and a half-built car in front of it. Define the end as the spot-welding of certain areas of the car. According to the definition above, any of the basic repertoire of arm movements is an available means. A way consisting of a causally integrated combination of such movements is also an available means. One of the movements results in the welding torch firing, and if there is a metal join suitably placed in front of the torch at that moment, an event of spot-welding will occur. The event of the torch welding the metal is not itself an available means, but if it is something which would happen given some suitable combination of movements that is an available means, then it can be incorporated in one. So, spot-welding a join in a certain location is an available means for the robot. So also is spot-welding a combination of such joins in succession.

I make no assumption that the means must be in the control of an agent. This will turn out to be a consequence of the means being available to a theoretical method of means-end justification that does explain something. A method of means-end justification that

---

[3] This notion of a basic repertoire is found in Danto (1973: ch. 5).

included as a possible means the process of lightning striking things would fail to represent any mechanism. So there is no agent (with the possible exception of Thor) for whom lightning striking would count as a means. If the method of means-end justification which included the robot arm movements as means did represent the functioning of some mechanism, then such movements would be potential actions. Different methods of practical justification will operate with different repertoires of basic activity. As far as the method of practical justification is concerned, almost any repertoire of basic activity is allowed. What constrains the repertoire is the question of whether such a method describes an actual mechanism.

The details of this account of agency will be provided in Chapter 5. All I want to show now is that I do not have to smuggle in a notion of agency in order to talk about means and ends. What is required instead is that a method of means-ends analysis be regarded as relative to a repertoire of basic activity.

D. EVOLUTIONARY EXPLANATION

My general approach to teleological explanation is externalistic, though I will wait till the next chapter to argue for this. This suggests that I might be able to accept the claim that evolutionary explanation is teleological without being committed to creationism. On the other hand, I want to argue that genuine teleological explanation is sufficient for agency. My Teleological Theory of Action states that whenever some activity is teleologically explainable that activity constitutes action. So, after all, to avoid having to think of Mother Nature as responsible for actions, I had better find a way of denying that evolutionary explanation is teleological. In this section I want to show that there is one sense in which evolutionary explanation is teleological and one sense in which it is not.

There is one argument against evolutionary explanation which is quite widely accepted, though I think incorrect. A version of this argument is expressed by B. F. Skinner (1953: 90):

A spider does not possess the elaborate behavioral repertoire with which it constructs a web because that web will enable it to capture the food it needs to survive. It possesses this behavior because similar behavior on the part of spiders in the past has enabled *them* to capture the food *they* needed to survive. A series of events have been relevant to the behavior of web-making in its earlier evolutionary history. We are wrong in saying that we observe the 'purpose' of the web when we observe similar events in the life of the individual.

I think that this sort of argument is behind a lot of recent criticism of teleological accounts of evolutionary explanation, and consequently of biological functions. A common way to describe one of the main oppositions in the philosophical treatment of biological functions is as an opposition between etiological and non-etiological accounts. According to etiological accounts, in order to tell whether some feature has a certain function, one must consider how that feature got there. Philosophers like Larry Wright and Ruth Millikan are regarded as etiologists. Those, like Robert Cummins and Christopher Boorse, who deny that the causal history of a feature is relevant to what function it has, are non-etiologists.

My concern is not with this opposition, however. For the sake of argument, I will side with the etiological theory of biological functions. My concern is with how such an etiological account might be spelt out. So I want to focus on the division between Wright and Millikan in their treatments of functions. This division does not primarily concern the notion of function at all; rather it concerns whether the evolutionary explanation of the presence of something in terms of the function it serves is a *teleological* explanation or a merely *historical* explanation. Roughly speaking, those philosophers who accept something like Skinner's argument think that it must be historical.

Larry Wright (1976: 78–9) argues for what he calls an etiological account in the following way:

Artifacts turn out to be good for all sorts of things that are not their functions. Dimmer switches are sometimes good for scratching your toe, sweep-second hands may keep the dust off the numerals, banking levers often make a good place to hang your hat. By contrast, the *function* of something is the *particular* thing that it is good for, which gives the proper insight into its etiology; it's what explains why it is there.

There are two features to this account. The first is the means-end requirement that if something has Z as a function it must be a means to the end of achieving Z—it must be good for Z. The second feature is the etiological requirement that whether or not something has a certain function depends on the explanation of why it is there. In particular, the explanation of why it is there must be in terms of the fact that it is a means to the end of achieving Z— the feature is there because it is good for Z. This part of Wright's account ties in pretty closely with the Aristotelian conception of teleological explanation.

Larry Wright goes on to spell this out as follows (1976: 81):

The function of X is Z iff:
  (i) Z is a consequence (result) of X's being there,
  (ii) X is there because it does (results in) Z.

So Wright's is a teleological account in which a feature has a function if and only if the presence of that feature can be explained in terms of what it is good for. If hearts are present because they are good for pumping blood, then, according to Wright, the function of hearts is to pump blood. Millikan denies this. Her account, though superficially similar to a teleological account, is crucially different. For Millikan, what a feature is good for is not relevant to whether or not it has a function. It is what *predecessors* of that feature *were* good for that is relevant. So, if our hearts are present because our ancestors' hearts were good for pumping blood, then, according to Millikan, the function of our hearts is to pump blood. It is not a teleological explanation of the presence of our hearts that is relevant to their having a function, but a non-teleological, historical explanation.

In Millikan's treatment of proper functions, she starts off with the same intuitive idea as Wright's. 'A function F is a direct proper function of x if x exists having character C because by having C it *can* perform F' (1984: 26). But she goes on to say: 'First interpret "because by having C it *can* perform F" to mean "because there were things that performed F in the past due to having C."' Elsewhere she writes (1993: 33): 'If it is to be causal, the "because there is something it can do" must be an elliptical reference to something past and to something once done.'

I think that the claim that 'because there is something it can do' might be an elliptical reference to something past and once done is obviously untenable. The claim is that a statement about the present is shorthand for a statement about the past. But the statement that my appendix can help with the digestion of food is not a shorthand for the statement that appendixes in the past helped with the digestion of food. The first statement is false and the second is true. So Millikan's account, despite its superficial similarity, should not be thought of as an interpretation of Wright's account. According to Millikan, it is not the case that a feature has a function in virtue of its presence being explicable in terms of what it is for the sake of.

Let me call Millikan's account causal-historical as opposed to Wright's causal-teleological account. Millikan, despite claiming that her account is an interpretation of the intuitive idea which is at the heart of Wright's account, at other times stresses the difference between a causal-historical account and a causal-teleological one (1993: 24 n. 5). But most philosophers working in this area ignore this difference. For example, Ernest Nagel (1977: 283-4) thinks that Wright's explanation of the function of President Ford's heart would be the following: 'President Ford has a beating heart in his body, because his ancestors had beating hearts that circulated their blood—a circumstance that gave them an advantage for survival.' This is despite the fact that Larry Wright himself explicitly rejects the causal-historical approach (1976: 88-90).

Similarly, Bigelow and Pargetter (1987: 187), while regarding Wright as the leading exponent of the etiological approach, describe it as a causal-historical theory as follows: 'Roughly, a character has a certain function when it has evolved, by natural selection, *because* it has had the effects that constitute the exercise of that function.' Neander (1991: 168) assumes the same sort of causal-historical reading of the etiological account.

Possibly these philosophers feel that they are being charitable to Wright. They may think that his stated position that something has a function in virtue of its presence being causally explicable in terms of what it does rather than what its predecessors did is so obviously wrong that it should not be taken seriously. However, Wright himself does take it very seriously, and I shall argue that he is correct to do so.

Larry Wright himself defends the account against the claims made in the quotation from Skinner about spiders' webs (1976: 87-90). But this defence has largely been ignored in the literature, and the same sort of claim keeps cropping up as if it was obvious to anyone who understood evolutionary theory that there is no genuine teleology in nature. So I think it is worthwhile to spell out a defence along the lines of Wright's in some detail.

Wright concedes that the presence of a web-making ability in a particular spider, call him Horatio, cannot be teleologically explained in terms of what functions that particular web-making ability serves. The process resulting in Horatio's web-making ability is not sensitive to whether or not that particular mechanism in Horatio serves a function. If making webs was no good for Horatio but some other ability was the way to catch flies he would still have the ability to make webs and he would not have this other ability.

Another point that could be conceded by Wright is that there is no process resulting in web-making being a feature of the *species* to which Horatio belongs which is sensitive to whether or not having web-making as a feature of the species serves a function. It is not the case that web-making is a feature of the species because it serves a function for web-making to be a feature of the species. Perhaps, having web-making as a feature of the species serves the function of the species not becoming extinct. But the evolutionary process which results in web-making becoming and being maintained as a feature of the species is not sensitive to this. If the species needed to have some other feature in order to survive, it would not get it. Only if the feature also served the survival interests of the individuals in the species would it become present.

The teleological claim that Larry Wright thinks he is entitled to make is different from both of these. He thinks that it is right to say that 'spiders possess the ability to spin webs because web-spinning helps catch food' (1976: 88). This is a sort of combination of the two claims just rejected. According to this claim, it is the presence of the web-making ability in the biological group rather than in the individual which is being explained. But it is being explained not in terms of the presence of the ability in the biological group being a means to an end, but in terms of the presence of the ability in an individual being a means to an end. The explanation is teleological because the presence of a feature is explained in terms of its presence being a means to an end. But it is more weakly teleological than explanation of purposive action, because it is not the case that something is being explained in terms of *it itself* being a means to an end. The presence of the feature in the biological group is not the same thing as the presence of the feature in an individual. The former is being explained in terms of what the latter is good for.

If I am right about the way to avoid deviant causal chain objections, Wright's claim should be spelt out in terms of processes. So the claim is that there is a process resulting in the web-spinning ability becoming and being maintained as a feature of the spider population which works in a way which is sensitive to the question of whether this feature serves the function of catching food for members of that population. If there is such a process it is teleological as it results in the presence of whatever feature serves some function.

Most writers on the subject think that it is obvious that there are no such explanations in nature, and that the process of evolution works differently. Millikan (1993: 26 n. 7) is particularly scathing:

Wright says that the formulation 'because X does Z' does *not* reduce to 'because things like X have done Z in the past' (pp. 89–90). Rather, we are asked to accept that X might be there *now* because it is true that *now* X does or Xs do result in Z. How the truth of a proposition about the present can 'cause' something else to be the case *at present* is not explained.

Part of this criticism just misses the point. When Wright says that X is present because X does Z, that X does Z is not supposed to be a fact about the present moment, but is supposed to be a timeless fact. It is like the fact that massive bodies attract one another. The present tense of the verb is used in stating this fact, not because the truth of the statement depends on the present moment, but because the truth of the statement is independent of what time it is. To use Wright's phrase, the sentence: 'X does Z' picks out a 'general property of a class' (1976: 90). When I say that the earth is accelerating towards the sun right now because massive bodies attract one another, I am not suggesting that the truth of a proposition about the present can cause something else to be the case at present. So it is with the claim that a web-making ability is present in spiders because having a web-making ability enables a spider to catch flies.

Having made the proviso that 'X does Z' is to be construed as a general property of a class, Wright is under some obligation to spell out which class and how general a property it is. I do not think that Wright discharges this obligation, so I will make some attempt to do so myself. But in spelling this out, one must be very careful to avoid a trap that Millikan sets (1993: 26–8).

Millikan asks the question: if having a web-making ability serves a function for members of the spider population by enabling them to catch flies, which members of the spider population must it serve the function for? It seems clear that it cannot be all members.

Having a web-making ability does not serve a function for all spiders, even for all spiders in web-making species. Clearly the process of evolution is not sensitive to whether something is true for every member of a species. So should we just require that it serves a function for *normal* members of the species? Millikan argues that we would then need to spell out what constitutes normality. Normal members cannot just be average members nor optimally placed members. It is easy to construct counter-examples for either of these two interpretations. Millikan claims that some reference to previous members is required to spell out the notion; and so a historical account of the means-end relation is required. This leads to her position that the claim that a web-making ability enables spiders to catch flies must be cashed out as a claim about previous spiders being enabled to catch flies by having a web-making ability.

Larry Wright does not say very much to help here. But I think that it is possible to construct a response to these objections which is entirely in line with his teleological account. First of all, I think that one must agree with Millikan that it is not a general property of the class of *spiders* that web-making serves a function for members of that class, where the word 'spider' has its usual biological meaning. It is not even a general property of web-making species of spiders. Furthermore, I do not think that it is right to say that it is a general property of the class in virtue of being a property of normal members of the class. These classes are defined in terms of biological family, and there is no sense, not even a historical one, in which, for all normal members of a biological family, web-making serves a function. This is because whether or not web-making serves a function for a spider depends partly on the environment. If there were no flying insects, web-making would not serve a function for a spider however normal it was.

The moral of this is that the class for whose members some feature serves a function should not be defined solely as the members of a biological family. The relevant class should be partly defined in terms of an environment. Rather than saying that evolution results in a feature becoming present and being maintained in a *species* or an *order*, we should say that it results in a feature becoming present and being maintained in a population which is individuated partly by certain environmental features. In the case of spiders, the population might be defined as follows: small wingless invertebrates which live in an area with shrubs and trees, whose prey are small flying insects, whose predators are . . . , etc. It is a fact about those environmental and other details that, for any organism which satisfies them, having a web-making ability is a means to the end of getting food. There is no need to invoke the notion of normal members of the population. If the population is defined intensionally in terms of certain characteristics (not including the feature being explained nor the result it is supposed to be a means to) and the environmental niche, then it is a general fact about the population as a whole that certain features serve certain functions for its members. It is also a timeless fact. One does not have to look at particular members of the population to establish it; one looks instead at the definition of the population.

There are two aspects to this suggestion. The first concerns how we should construe the claim that some feature being a means to an end is a *general property of a class*. That is that we should be working with a notion of a class or a population which is defined intensionally by a set of properties and not extensionally by a list of its members. The properties need to be sufficiently temporally precise that if an individual satisfies one such property at a time, then it always does. For example, rather than defining a spider by the property of having flying insects in its environment, we should use the property of having flying insects in its environment *for some of its life*. This means that the notion of a population that I am envisaging is not that of a shifting population with individuals moving in and out of the same population as they acquire and lose temporally unspecific properties.

The fact that a feature is a means to an end for the members of a population as I am using the notion of a population is a fact about the properties that define that population. Of course, it is also a fact about all the members of the population; but in order to establish that this fact holds, there is no need to look at every member of the population and check that the feature is a means to an end for them.

The second aspect of my suggestion concerns the properties that define the sort of population we are working with when making a teleological claim about biology. It is not good enough to define a population merely in terms of biological families. If the claim that some feature is a means to an end for members of a population is to be a general fact about that population, the definition of the population must narrow it down more than this. I am suggesting that properties of the environmental niche should be included along with intrinsic properties of the organism. Then there is some prospect that a sufficiently narrow definition of a population can be arrived at that it follows from the definition alone that the feature in question is a means to an end for all members of that population.

The possibility of convergent evolution suggests that the populations that teleological evolution works on should be defined by other properties in addition to intrinsic and environmental properties. When two unrelated but morphologically identical types of tree develop aerial roots as a way of coping with life in tidal estuaries, we want to say that there are two distinct evolutionary processes happening here, though they work in the same sort of way. So there should be a way of defining the populations which distinguishes between them. It would be a mistake to include the *species* of tree in the definition of the population since trees would not be members of the relevant species if they did not have aerial roots. But I can see no objection to including some specification of lineage as one of the properties defining the population.

So, for example, we might define one population by the following properties:

1. Belonging to species, S (where S is the name of a species of mangrove tree), or a recent ancestor species of S.
2. Inhabiting at some stage of its life an environmental niche, E (where E specifies such things as being a tree of a certain size taking root in tidal estuaries, etc.).

Something is a member of the designated population if it satisfies these properties. For anything which satisfies all these properties, having aerial roots serves the function of stopping the plant from being washed away by tides. (If this is not the function of aerial roots in mangrove trees, then the correct function should be substituted here.) If a counter-example can be thought of where, because some tree might have or lack some key property, having aerial roots does not serve this function for it despite it satisfying the properties that define the population, then lacking or having this key property should be included as one of the properties defining the population. The definition of the population can be made more and more detailed until it really follows from the definition alone that there is a function such that for any member of the population, having aerial roots serves that function.

So, I think that there is no objection in principle to constructing definitions of populations which will ensure that the first part of Wright's account, the means-end requirement, is satisfied in nature. It should always be possible to define a population in such a way that it follows just from that definition that some feature is a means to an end for members of that population. The definition will be partly morphological, partly environmental, and partly in terms of lineage.

But what of the second part of Wright's account? Does evolution work in a way which is sensitive to facts about what is a means to an end for members of some population? I think that it does. If the environment partly defining a certain population of spiders was such that for things which inhabited that environment and satisfied the various other properties defining the population, some other feature served the function of enabling them to get food and various background conditions held, then that other feature would become present in the population so defined. If the environment that partly defined the relevant population of spiders was such that there were no shrubs or trees, then having a web-making ability would not be much good for things which inhabited that environment, but being a very strong jumper might be. Suppose also that various background conditions, including the genetic availability of the new feature, held. In this case, evolution would indeed result in the feature of being a very strong jumper becoming present in that population.

This claim might seem excessively adaptationist to some philosophers of biology. It would not do my defence of Wright's teleological account any harm if a weak version of adaptationism was all we were entitled to, as long as it sanctioned the claim that the presence of a trait in a population is sometimes explained by the usefulness of that trait. Moderate anti-adaptationists generally argue that sometimes the presence of a trait in a population cannot be explained in terms of the usefulness of that trait (e.g. Gould and Lewontin 1979). But they do not argue that this is the case for all traits. As far as the present argument between Millikan and Wright is concerned, it is probably enough to note that Millikan herself resists a wholesale attack on adaptationism (1993: ch. 2). If wholesale anti-adaptationism were correct, then Wright's notion of a biological function would be empty; but then so would Millikan's.

It might be objected that there is something fishy about a causal process being sensitive to *general* facts about environmental niches, etc. Proper processes, it might be thought, should respond to historical events, not such facts. But stated this baldly, this sounds like mere prejudice. Sensitivity of a mechanism to different conditions is often manifested in the different responses of that mechanism to different events impinging on that mechanism. But it might equally be manifested in different responses of that mechanism to different environments in which it is placed. In this case, given that mechanism, facts about the environment, even necessarily true facts, are as much to be counted as causal influences on what happens as are the events in the first case.

Moreover, there is a feature of the process of evolution that might mean that it is necessary to use general rather than historical facts in evolutionary explanations. That is that evolution explains continuous phenomena rather than precise historical facts. Evolution explains why features become present and are maintained in populations, and so it is quite appropriate to cite general rather than temporally precise facts in the explanation.

An example might make this clearer. Consider the explanation of why large stones rise to the surface of fields. Suppose that the field is constantly being shaken up by the action of earthworms, etc. Large stones, in virtue of being large, do not fall through the gaps between small stones as much as small stones fall through the gaps between large stones. So, overall, large stones end up on top and stay on top. It is better to cite the general fact that small stones *fall* through gaps between large stones rather than the historical fact that small stones *fell* through gaps between large stones for two reasons. The first is that the general fact is more explanatory—it is needed in order to explain the historical fact. The second is that the process being described is a continuous process. We do not want just to explain the state of the field at a particular moment. We want to explain the continuing fact that more and more large stones rise to the surface and stay there.

If Wright's account as I have tried to explicate it is correct, there is something misleading in telling a child that she has eyes so that she can see things, rather than saying that *we* have eyes so that we can see things. If there is a sense in which it is right to say that the particular child has eyes so that she can see things, it is right in virtue of the child belonging to a population which has members with eyes because having eyes enables the members of that population to see things. What makes it true that we have eyes so that we can see is not that Jenny has eyes so that she can see, and so on with each person. Rather it is the other way around. What makes it true that Jenny has eyes so that she can see is that she is one of us; and we have eyes so that we can see. And similarly, if it is right to say that Jenny's eyes have a biological function, then it is right in virtue of it being true that eyes for some population of creatures which includes her have a biological function.

It is this which enables Wright's account to deal effectively with the possibility of defective organs. These are organs which have a function for a population but fail to serve that function for some unfortunate member of that population. Consider, for example, a diabetic's pancreas. We want to be able to say that such a pancreas is defective, since it fails to serve the function it is there for. So this seems to be a case where an organ has a function but does not serve that function. Millikan (1993: 21–3) thinks that the only way that we can account for this is by assigning a function to the pancreas in virtue of the function served by predecessors of that pancreas. But this is not so. According to Wright's account, the diabetic's pancreas has a function in virtue of pancreases in members of one of the diabetic's populations having a function; and this fact is derived from the definition of the population, not generalized from particular members of it. It is a general fact about our environmental niche that an insulin-producing pancreas would serve a function for inhabitants of it. This is why members of that population including the diabetics have pancreases. But, although the diabetics have pancreases, they do not have insulin-producing pancreases; so their pancreases do not in practice serve the function that they are there for.

Although Millikan and Wright both attribute functions in virtue of causal explanations, the relevant explanandum is different for the two accounts. Millikan takes a particular token of a feature and explains its presence in terms of its being the offspring of ancestors of that token feature which only reproduced themselves because they served a function. Wright takes a type of feature and explains its presence or prevalence in a population in terms of its serving a function for members of that population. This is not an explanation of the presence of a particular token of that feature. Whether it is even the *basis* for an explanation of the presence of a particular token of the feature is brought into serious doubt by the arguments for the distinction between selectional and developmental explanation propounded by Sober (1984) among others.

According to Wright's account, a particular token feature, like my kneecap, has a biological function only in virtue of belonging to a type of feature which has a function relative to a population in which it occurs. Its function is derivative. By contrast, particular tokens of handmade articles or of bits of purposive behaviour may have functions in virtue of explanations of why those tokens are present in terms of their serving some function.

According to Millikan's account, my kneecap may have a function in virtue of some causal explanation of that very token. This has the advantage of enabling us to construct an account of organ types in terms of the functions of the tokens that fall under these types. For example, we might want to say that my kneecap counts as a kneecap and the same sort of thing as your kneecap in virtue of the function it has. But this is not a decisive factor in favour of Millikan's account, since there are other ways of accounting for organ types. For example, a kneecap may be characterized in terms of morphological details or in terms of how it functions (as opposed to what its function is).

What is the telling advantage of Wright's teleological account of functions is that it saves a place for teleology in nature, while not sacrificing a straightforwardly naturalistic causal approach to functions. Our intuitive conception of biological functions has this teleological component, and although this conception could be revised in the light of a better understanding of evolutionary theory, if there is a way of saving it, this way should be followed.

The conclusion I have reached concerning evolutionary explanation is that it is teleological in a sense, though not in the strongest sense. We can say that a feature becoming present and being maintained in a population is explained in terms of the fact that the presence of that feature in a member of that population is a means to an end. We can loosely say that the presence of the feature is explained in terms of the fact that the presence of that feature is a means to an end. But the phrase, 'the presence of the feature', picks out something different in the two places it occurs in that sentence. In the first instance, it picks out the presence of the feature in a population; in the second instance, it picks out the presence of the feature in a member of the population. What we cannot say in a case of evolutionary explanation is that the occurrence of some type of activity is explained in terms of that very type of activity being a means to an end. So, strictly speaking, in evolutionary explanation, we do not have cases of a thing happening because *it* should. We have cases of a thing happening because something else, very closely related, should.

Let me describe as strong teleological explanation, explanation of the occurrence of activity of some type in terms of the occurrence of activity of that very type being a means to an end. If activity which constitutes intentional action is teleologically explained, it is strongly teleologically explained. If my hand's moving in a certain way is teleologically explained, it is explained in terms of my hand's moving in that way being a means to an end. It is not explained in terms of, say, some other person's hand moving in that way being a means to an end. Given this notion, the Teleological Theory of Action described in Chapter 1 had better be phrased in terms of strong teleological explanation. For we do not want the results of evolution to be classed as intentional actions.

E. SMART THERMOSTATS

There are various other sorts of activity which fall short of constituting intentional actions, but which might be thought to be strongly teleologically explained. It might be thought that the automatic activity of certain body organs occurs for the sake of some ends. Similarly, it might be thought that the instinctive behaviour of animals is teleologically explained, but is not action. Or, the apparently goal-directed activity of 'smart' computerized systems might be thought to occur for the sake of their programmed goals, though not be intentional action. If the Teleological Theory of Action is to provide a sufficient condition, a way had better be found to show why such cases are not genuine cases of strong teleological explanation.

Let me start with the traditional thermostat. Its activity might loosely be described as directed to keeping a room at a certain temperature. Is its activity teleologically explained? On the face of it, the way the mechanism works is sensitive to what is the right way to keep the room temperature at approximately the right level. If the room temperature rises above the desired level, then the means to the end of the room being maintained at close to that level is for the heater to switch off. This is precisely what happens. Similarly, when the temperature goes below the desired level, the means to the same end is for the heater to switch on, and that is what happens too.

On the other hand, it seems anthropomorphic to say that the circuit closes *in order that* the room's temperature is maintained at approximately such-and-such a level. One thing that might be lacking from the thermostat is the right degree of flexibility or sensitivity. If you open a window beside the thermostat's thermocouple so that the thermocouple is colder than the room overall, even if switching off the heater is the way to maintain the overall room temperature at a certain level, it will not happen.

The thermostat has what Hofstadter (1982) and Dennett (1984: 10 ff.) call sphexishness. This property is named after the digger wasp, *Sphex Ichneumoneus*, which will persist in doing what, in normal circumstances, is the right thing to do, even in those circumstances where it is obviously the wrong thing to do. The activity of the thermostat and the wasp usually accords with what is the means to an end. But in circumstances that the thermostat was not designed to cope with or that the wasp's behavioural mechanisms were not selected to cope with, the activity does not accord with the same means-end justification.

There is an argument that is usually invoked at this point in the discussion, which I shall argue is an important mistake. It starts with the observation that the activity of people is not 100 per cent rational either; there will always be circumstances where the cleverest of us will produce activity which does not accord with means-end rationality. It is supposed to follow from this that in this respect the difference between us and wasps and thermostats is just one of degree. We are a lot more reliably rational and adaptable than them. It seems to follow that if it is right to explain our behaviour teleologically, then it is also right to explain their behaviour teleologically. The only difference is that the predictions that go with the teleological explanation in their case are less reliable.

My account of explanation shows what is wrong with this argument and allows us to maintain a clear-cut distinction between us and thermostats and wasps in which our activity is teleologically explained and theirs cannot be, even a little bit.

First of all, there is no need for a mechanism to be reliable in order for it to be correct to describe it as resulting in some structure of stages. All that is required is that there are some extra conditions—the activation conditions of the mechanism—such that when they accompany the mechanism, the structure of stages *always* follows (see Chapter 2, Section B). How commonly those activation conditions are realized is not relevant. A teleological mechanism might only rarely be activated, but that would not stop it from being a teleological mechanism. Similarly, the ability to predict that the structure of stages follows from the presence of the mechanism is quite irrelevant to the question of whether the mechanism results in that structure of stages. All this follows from the analysis of Chapter 2.

Applying this analysis to the thermostat, there is no difficulty in saying that the thermostat is a mechanism which results in the room being maintained at some temperature level approximately. The activation conditions include the condition that the temperature is approximately uniform throughout the room. If the temperature by the thermocouple is much lower than the temperature in the rest of the room, then the mechanism for keeping the overall room temperature at a certain level will not be working properly. But, if the condition of temperature uniformity is satisfied along with other activation conditions, then the characteristic results of the room temperature being kept at a certain level will occur.

The situation is subtly, but crucially, different if we ask whether the thermostat is a mechanism whose results are in conformity with a *means-end justification* where the end is keeping the overall room temperature at a certain level. At first sight, it is hard to see how there can be a difference between the thermostat resulting in the means to the end of keeping the room at some temperature and the thermostat resulting in the room being kept at that temperature. Resulting in the means to the end of keeping the room at some temperature is both necessary and sufficient for resulting in the room being kept at that temperature. But it does not follow that a mechanism that results in a room being kept at a certain temperature is automatically a mechanism that results in the means to the end of the room being kept at that temperature. This is because there is a difference in what activation conditions can belong with the two mechanisms when their characteristic stages are described in these ways.

In particular, it cannot be one of the activation conditions of a mechanism which characteristically results in the means to the end of keeping the room at a certain temperature that the temperature be approximately uniform throughout the room. The situation in which the temperature in the vicinity of the thermocouple is 5 degrees cooler than that of the rest of the room is a situation in which the method of means-end justification gives a special result for what should happen—namely that the heater should be switched on or off when the thermocouple is 5 degrees cooler than the required temperature. The problem with allowing activation conditions for this mechanism which exclude this situation altogether is that such activation conditions would exclude part of the characteristic structure of stages of the mechanism. This means that the description of the characteristic stages of the mechanism would include too much and would have to be reduced accordingly.

The general point here is that a mechanism should not be so characterized that the activation conditions required for the mechanism to be working properly exclude part of the structure of stages described by that characterization. The point can be illustrated by more obvious examples. Suppose that I have programmed a computer to work in the following way. Given any input of an integer in the range 0 to 10, that same integer will be output unless the input is 2 in which case there is no output; for any other input (including no input at all) nothing will be output. Would the following describe a mechanism at work here? 'Given any input of an integer in the range 0 to 10 that same integer is output; for any other input there is no output.' In other words, can we include among the activation conditions of the mechanism the fact that 2 is not input along with other requirements like the machine being switched on, etc.?

The answer is no. The theoretical method that is supposed to represent the way the mechanism works discriminates between situations in which different integers are input. The method represents the mechanism only if there is a way of the mechanism working (the underlying nature of the mechanism working includes its activation conditions being satisfied) which results in what is described by the theoretical method in all the types of situation discriminated by that method. But there is no way of the mechanism working—no set of activation conditions—where in addition to outputting all the other results described by the method, it also outputs 2 when 2 is input.

A more extreme example would be that of describing a normal

stone as a mechanism for turning lead into gold while leaving other metals unchanged. We cannot allow that one of the activation conditions of such a mechanism be that there is no lead in the vicinity.

The principle I am invoking here provides a constraint on appropriate theoretical methods for describing processes. The principle is that the theoretical method should not discriminate between situations more finely than the process does. No distinctions made by the theoretical method should turn out to be redundant. If a theoretical method does discriminate more finely than a process does, then it is not a proper description of that process.

In the case of a theoretical method embodying means-end justification which is supposed to describe the way a thermostat works, there is no explicit reference to the uniformity of the temperature in the room. Nevertheless, the method does discriminate at this level. It leads to different descriptions of what should happen in situations where the temperature close to the thermocouple is 5 degrees lower than the overall room temperature and in those where the temperature is uniform throughout the room. This is in contrast with the theoretical method which does not embody means-end justification but just leads to the description that the room will remain at such-and-such a temperature. This second method leads to exactly the same description of what should happen in those situations where the room temperature is not uniform and in those where it is. Given this second method, no discrimination is lost by requiring in the activation conditions of the mechanism whose working is described by it that the room temperature be uniform.

The problem with describing the way a thermostat works with a theoretical method embodying means-end justification is that such a method is too discriminating. But it should be possible to restrict such a method so that it is less discriminating. For example, we might describe the way a thermostat works by saying that its results conform with means-end justification given the end of keeping the room at such-and-such a temperature and given that the room temperature is uniform. This last clause means that the method of describing the mechanism does not give a special result in situations where the temperature in the vicinity of the thermocouple is lower than the overall room temperature.

By itself this restriction is insufficient. Even given that the temperature of the room is initially uniform, there is an indefinite number of other ways that the situation can be altered so that the thermostat's programmed activity is not the means to the designated end. For example, if the room is about to be filled with some hot objects, then the right way to keep the temperature at the required level might be to switch off the heater early. The activity of the thermostat fails to conform with this course.

Is there a way of restricting a theoretical method embodying means-end justification so that *all* such problematic situations are excluded from consideration by the method? I think not. First of all, consider the following claim.

> There is no specification of a type of situation such that it is universally true to say that in such situations the means to the end *E* is *M*, where *E* and *M* are independently specified.

If this claim is true, then it is not possible to specify a set of restrictions such that within those restrictions the means to keeping the room at such-and-such a temperature is always to switch on and off the heater when the temperature at the thermocouple is such-and-such. So, there would be no way to construct a theoretical method embodying a restricted form of means-end justification which correctly described how the thermostat works.

It could be argued that the claim is false since a list of the states of all the elementary particles within some appropriate light cone in situations in which the thermostat does result in keeping the room at the designated temperature would be a specification of a type of situation in which it is universally true to say that the means to the end of keeping the room at the designated temperature is for the heater to be switched on and off when the thermocouple is at that temperature. One thing wrong with this argument is that it contradicts the uncertainty principle of quantum mechanics. But, even if such a specification could be drawn up, a theoretical method would be so weighed down by it that the means-end component of the method could no longer be regarded as significant.

Another way to describe the way a thermostat works would be to say that it results in the means to the end of keeping the room at such-and-such a temperature in those situations where the means is to switch the heater on and off when the thermocouple is at such-and-such a temperature. The trouble with this is that all reference to means and ends is entirely redundant in this description; the description is logically equivalent to one where there is no mention of means and ends.

It is important to see that it is not just the simplicity of a thermostat's response that stops it from being teleological. Consider a 'smart' thermostat like the one described by Dennett (1987: ch. 2). Let it include multiple input devices and robotic output devices. Let it be programmed with a series of rules and allow it to derive the logical consequences of these rules. This thermostat would be very much more adaptable than the simple one. But, given the claim above, that there is no specification (and certainly none manageable enough to be programmed into a computer) of a type of situation such that in *all* such situations the means to E is M, there is no way of making the thermostat completely adaptable. It will always by possible to bring out its sphexishness in some set of conditions which could not all be ruled out by appropriate activation conditions or restrictions on the scheme of means-end justification.

It might be a worry that if one is so hard on smart computers, people might not fare any better. It is always possible to construct evil demon scenarios in which a person is systematically deceived just as it is possible to construct such scenarios for digger wasps or smart thermostats. Does this show that our behaviour too is sphexish and not the result of a genuinely teleological process?

It is certainly the case that a scheme of practical justification describing how we work must be restricted in certain ways. But I think that in our case, unlike the case of the thermostat, there is a way of restricting the scheme of practical justification describing how we work so that it still essentially involves means-end justification. I will develop this thought over the next couple of chapters. But, roughly, the claim is that we work in the following way: if the means to some end is *apparent* and falls within some *repertoire* of activity, then it will result. What characterizes sphexishness is that there is some situation in which, however apparent it is to the system that the means to the end is such-and-such, and however much doing such-and-such falls within the repertoire of the system, it still does not do it. But with people, if you make it apparent enough what they need to do, then they will do it.

Drawing a sharp distinction between people and a certain kind of thermostat does not commit one to denying that machines can ever be teleological. The boom in parallel distributed processing—

PDP—provides us with machines which adapt their programs in the light of failures and successes (see Rumelhart and McLelland 1986; also Clark 1989). They are still not teleological, because they always react to past failures rather than working out in advance what is best. But, if you combine these with perceptual devices that actively test hypotheses in the process of gleaning information as well as internal trial and error processes, I think teleology will start to seem attainable.

One thing which distinguishes PDP systems from old-fashioned expert systems like the smart thermostat is that the interesting properties that we can attribute to them are *emergent* properties. What this means is that these properties are not programmed into the system, but instead turn out to be part of the system as it evolves. This ability to evolve to deal with new situations is what opens up the possibility that if you make it apparent enough to a PDP system what it needs to do, then it might do it. A programmed property is always limited by the program; its sphexishness can always be revealed by setting up a situation not covered by the program. An emergent property is not so limited.

All this contradicts the influential view of Dennett (1987: ch. 2) that there is no way to make such a clear-cut distinction between us and thermostats. This view derives from the way he construes the role of what he calls the intentional stance or the intentional strategy. What Dennett calls the intentional stance is very like what I call a theoretical method embodying means-end justification. He describes it as follows (1987: 17):

Here is how it [the intentional stance] works: first you decide to treat the object whose behaviour is to be predicted as a rational agent; then you figure out what beliefs that agent ought to have, given its place in the world and its purpose. Then you figure out what desires it ought to have, on the same considerations, and finally you predict that this rational agent will act to further its goals in the light of its beliefs. A little practical reasoning from the chosen set of beliefs and desires will in many—but not all—instances yield a decision about what the agent ought to do; that is what you predict the agent *will* do.

I will argue in the next chapter that you do not need to include reference to the agent's beliefs and desires in such a method, but that is not the crucial difference between my position and Dennett's at this stage. The crucial difference is that, for Dennett, what determines whether or not the intentional stance works in any particular case is to what degree it successfully *predicts* the agent's activity, whereas, for me, it is to what degree it successfully *explains* the agent's activity. I have been arguing in Chapter 2 that this is a quite different requirement.

Dennett writes (1987: 29):

The perverse claim remains: *all there is* to being a true believer is being a system whose behaviour is reliably predictable via the intentional strategy, and hence *all there is* to really and truly believing that *p* (for any proposition *p*) is being an intentional system for which *p* occurs as a belief in the best (most predictive) interpretation.

He also claims (1987: 22) that the intentional strategy works to a greater or lesser degree for birds, thermostats, and plants, and moreover it does not work perfectly for people (1987: 28). Putting all this together gives us his view that what makes it right to attribute rational purposiveness to ourselves also makes it right, though to a lesser degree, to attribute it to thermostats, etc. Where he has gone wrong, in my view, is to concentrate on the *predictive* power of the intentional stance. I can see no reason to suppose this to be relevant. What we should be interested in is whether the intentional stance represents the way we actually work. If my account of explanation works then the predictive usefulness of a method is independent of whether it correctly describes what is happening. If is it impossible to predict whether the activation conditions of some teleological mechanism are satisfied then the intentional stance will not be a good predictive tool even when it correctly describes what is happening.

My treatment of thermostats, if it works at all, should work equally well for body organs. Consider the process which maintains the blood-sugar level in one's body within a certain range. Very roughly, the pancreas produces more or less insulin in response to the concentration of sugar in the bloodstream, and the liver responds to the concentration of insulin by metabolizing more or less sugar. This process is homoeostatic and can loosely be described as directed to maintaining blood-sugar-level equilibrium. But, like the process of a thermostat regulating a room's temperature, this process is not really teleological at all.

Suppose that a situation arises where something other than the normal response of the pancreas is required to keep blood-sugar at the correct level. Perhaps a massive secretion of insulin is required right away to cope with the injection of a strong glucose solution into your bloodstream that will be made in a few minutes. Your pancreas will respond to the injection after it is made, but this will be too late. The only way to stop the blood-sugar level from rising to a fatal level is for the pancreas to start working now, which of course it will not do.

I have argued that there is no requirement that the mechanisms underlying processes be 100 per cent reliable. Things may interfere with the structure of a mechanism so that the process is not happening and the characteristic results fail to materialize. So, there is no problem with the thought that the characteristic result of the process controlling the blood-sugar level fails to materialize because there is something lacking in the underlying mechanism in this case. Part of the underlying nature of this process is that any externally created imbalances in the blood-sugar level are not greater than a certain amount. This condition is not satisfied. If all such conditions were satisfied, then the process resulting in the blood-sugar level being in the correct range would be happening.

But it is a very different story if we consider the question of whether it is a characteristic result of this process that a *means* to the end of achieving the correct blood-sugar level is achieved. In the situation being considered, neither the process of achieving the correct blood-sugar level nor the process of achieving a means to the end of achieving the correct blood-sugar level is happening. If the latter process were happening in this case, it would result in the early secretion of insulin. Now, although the operating conditions can be improved so that the process of achieving the correct blood-sugar level is happening, there is no way of improving the conditions so that the process of achieving a means to the end of achieving the correct blood-sugar level is happening. However one makes sure that all the activation conditions are in place and nothing is interfering, there is no way that the early secretion of insulin will result. The failure to achieve a means to the end of achieving the correct blood-sugar level cannot be attributed to some lack in the underlying conditions in this case or else there would be a way of remedying that failure so that the underlying conditions were fully present and the process was happening and achieved that result. But there is no way of characterizing the underlying conditions of the process in question in such a way that it results in a means to the end of achieving the correct blood-sugar level in this case.

Contrast this with the parallel case where human purpose is involved. Consider the process of a diabetic achieving a means to the end of keeping the correct blood-sugar level. We can construct similar examples where she fails to achieve the best way. But always it will be possible to attribute such failure to a lack in the underlying conditions of the process. For, in those circumstances where it is apparent to the diabetic agent that some activity, A, is the best way of achieving the correct blood-sugar level and her brain is working properly, then A will be done. The control mechanism of the diabetic agent may be much less reliable than the body's natural mechanism, but at least, when all its conditions are satisfied, its working can be described in terms of a means-ends justification.

4

Practical Justification

A. WHAT CHARACTERIZES PRACTICAL JUSTIFICATION

My starting-point in this book was a generalized version of the causal theory of action which I have called the Teleological Theory of Action. This says that activity constitutes action in virtue of being explainable in terms of a practical justification of it. My main task is to show that we can get this Teleological Theory of Action to work with a purely externalist conception of practical justification. Then I want to show that the availability of this externalist story for action is what constitutes agency, and that an account of intentional mental states can be derived from it.

In the previous chapter I have considered explanations of things in terms of means-end justifications of them. I called such explanations teleological explanations. I have tried to show that such explanations only apply to actions and not to the activity of wasps or current-day computers. The notion of means-end justification that I have been working with has been an externalist one; but I do not think that there is anything there that someone with an internalist conception of means-end justification need object to.

In this chapter I want to show that practical justification must involve means-end justification. This ties up the material in the previous chapter on teleological explanation with the Teleological Theory of Action. I also want to show that the kind of means-end justification that must be involved in practical justification is externalist.

A natural way to start to characterize practical justification is to say that, whereas theoretical justification is the justification of belief, practical justification is the justification of action. According to this starting-point, the 'character of an inference as a practical one is determined by the nature of its conclusion' (Raz 1978: 5). But I think that characterizing practical justification as inference to an action or to a description of an action is quite unhelpful, for several reasons.

First, this characterization says nothing useful about what characterizes justification in general. A justification is a way of deriving or inferring the conclusion that some result should happen. But not every such way counts as a justification. It is easy to think of theoretical methods which determine the conclusion that some action should occur, which are not themselves practical justifications. For example, it is said that people who have been bullied as children by their parents tend to bully their own children. There is a theoretical method describing this process, according to which, you should bully your children if you yourself have been bullied as a child. But this theoretical method does not provide a practical justification of bullying your children. There *is* a practical justification which often goes along with this process. It goes like this: 'My parents did it to me and it never did me any harm; so why shouldn't I do it to my kids.' But this is quite distinct from the theoretical method describing the merely psychological process.

The theoretical method describing the merely psychological process does not really justify the action at all. According to the Law of Gravity, an unsupported stone should fall to the ground; but the Law of Gravity does not justify the fall of the stone. So, even if the distinction between practical and theoretical justification could be characterized in terms of the different natures of their conclusions, the distinction between these and other kinds of theoretical method cannot be so characterized. Some additional account of justification is required.

This objection might be overcome by saying that practical justification determines a special kind of description of an action—namely an imperative or a 'should' statement. But there still remains the question of what is so special about methods which determine such descriptions. What would be wrong with framing the Law of Gravity in such a way that it issues imperatives to stones? Some more explanatory characterization is required.

The second main reason for finding this way of characterizing the special nature of practical justification unhelpful is that it presupposes a notion of action. Given the Teleological Theory of Action, it follows trivially that practical justifications are justifications of action. But the point of the Teleological Theory of Action is that it enables us to give an account of action in terms of the notion of practical justification, not the other way around. If only in the interests of keeping this project alive, it is important to try to find a more basic characterization of practical justification.

I think that it must be conceded that, even if there is a way of characterizing practical justification in terms of a special kind of theoretical method without referring to action, this is not an absolutely basic starting-point for an account of action. This is because a theoretical method is a way of deriving descriptions; it is a way of doing something. As such, it is a practical method too. However, although a theoretical method is a practical method in a sense, I do not think that one needs a notion of action in order to understand what a theoretical method is. One can understand that certain moves are dictated by the rules of a game without seeing those moves as actions. Similarly, I think that one can understand that certain descriptions are determined by a theoretical method without seeing those descriptions as the contents of linguistic *actions*. At any rate, it is with the notion of a theoretical method that my spade turns in this account.

B. NORMATIVITY

The first distinction I want to draw is between normative and non-normative theoretical methods. Let a normative theoretical method be one which justifies the thing that is described by that method as well as justifying the description of the thing. The Law of Gravity does not justify the fall of the stone, though it does justify the description of the fall of the stone; so it is not a normative theoretical method. On the other hand, some version of the laws of table-laying etiquette which say where each knife is to be placed does justify the little knife being placed to the right of the big knife as well as justifying the description that the little knife is placed to the right of the big knife. So the laws of table-laying etiquette constitute a normative method.

Suppose now that we make up some absurd aesthetic theory in which objects of a certain colour should remain suspended in the air when unsupported while other objects should fall to the ground; and suppose that a certain stone has this colour. According to this strange theory, the stone should remain suspended in the air when dropped. What is interesting is that this theory, despite being absurd, does something that the Law of Gravity does not do; it provides a norm or justification. The actual behaviour of the stone will contravene this norm; the stone will be doing the wrong thing according to this theory. By contrast, the behaviour of a differently coloured stone may be justified by this theory; such a stone will be doing the right thing by falling to the ground.

What seems to make some theoretical method a normative method of justification is that it is a way of deriving descriptions which is itself arrived at independently of describing the process which is actually happening. The point of normative assessment is to endorse or criticize something. So, there is no point in using the theoretical method which describes the actual process resulting in something to provide the norms assessing it. It is that process which is being assessed. On pain of triviality, its description should not be used as a way of assessing it.

Now we can see that the difference between a theoretical method which is and one which is not a normative method of assessment is not a difference in what they describe but a difference in how they are used and what they depend on. Suppose the behaviour of a stone fails to conform to some theoretical method. We might either accept that the theoretical method applies in this situation, and say that the stone has behaved badly; or we might say that the theoretical method has failed somehow—it does not correctly describe what happens. If we follow the first path, we are using the theoretical method as a normative method; if we follow the second, we are using it as a descriptive method. What characterizes the normative method is that its *own* correctness or incorrectness does not completely depend on how well it describes what happens.[1]

This raises an interesting problem when we move on to consider normative *explanation*—explanation of something in terms of its conformity to some normative method. For example, according to the Teleological Theory of Action, the fact that activity which constitutes action is normatively justified also explains why it happens. The problem is that, according to my account of processes, every single process results in things which some theoretical method says should happen. The theoretical method in such cases will be the description of the process. So, saying that a process results in things which some theoretical method says should happen does not

---

[1] As a complete theory of normativity, this would be hopelessly circular; but here I am just trying to sketch a distinction.

say anything that is characteristic of action. Saying this does not distinguish an action, like placing the little knife to the right of the big one, from an event, like the falling of a stone under gravity. What is required of a normative method is not just that it describes the results of the process, but that it is an *input* to this process.

Let N designate a normative method like the one consisting of some laws of table-laying etiquette and let P be a process which results in what is justified by N. Let D be a theoretical method describing P's results. The problem is how to distinguish between N and D so that N does not turn out to be *just* a description of P, but rather determines the inputs to P. This may be done if N can be identified independently of spelling out exactly what results should be derived according to N. For example, N might be partially identifiable in the practices of a linguistic community. Perhaps correct table-laying etiquette is partly constituted by what a certain group of table-laying authorities do. One might be able to point to some practice and say that that is N (correct table-laying etiquette, say) without being able to spell out what N yields in every situation. Indeed, if one accepts what Wittgenstein says about rule-following, it might be theoretically impossible to spell out what N yields in every situation.[2]

So, a normative method is not identified solely in terms of the set of recommendations it makes. What makes it normative is that it has some independent identity—some autonomy. This means that it makes sense to say that the same normative method might work in different ways. A normative method, unlike a strictly descriptive method, may evolve.

C. MEANS-END JUSTIFICATION

If it were theoretically possible to have an omnipotent agent, then this would constitute a counter-example to the claim that practical justification must involve means-end justification. Consider the possibility of a deliberator who can make any activity at all part of her basic activity. She decides what should be the case—perhaps not using instrumental thinking at all, but, say, aesthetic thinking. Then she says: 'Let it be so,' and it becomes so. Should we say

---

[2] This interpretation of Wittgenstein derives from McDowell (1987). There is a very useful discussion of the notion of normativity in Brandom (1994: ch. 1).

that the results of her deliberation are not to count as practically justified just because she is such an effective agent that she makes these results come about directly, with no need for indirect means?

This is clearly rather a difficult question to assess. But I do not see any philosophical reason to suppose the idea of an omnipotent *agent* to be a coherent one. If purely aesthetic judgements had a direct causal influence on the world, this would not be enough to make them practical justifications. Down on earth we might talk about things happening because they are beautiful. But, if none of these things happened because they led to anything else, then we would have no reason to think of them as *practically* justified.

What this divine deliberator lacks are practical constraints. It is the presence of practical constraints on what is justified that makes for practical justification. There is no natural process that can produce directly every result that is justified by some arbitrary independent normative method. Any natural process is constrained by a fixed repertoire of things that can directly result from it; that is what makes a normative method which is appropriate as an input for that process a practical method.

If the results of some normative method fall outside the repertoire of basic activity which a process can produce directly, yet the process results in what is justified by that method, then the process must *indirectly* produce those results. The process results in things which themselves result in the things described by the normative method—it results in the pieces of activity which achieve those things.

There are rather a lot of processes being described here; so I should try to disentangle the suggestion. Consider again the case of a method of table-laying etiquette governing someone's behaviour. The suggestion is that when there is a process governed by such a method, the following activity is happening. First of all there is the process which takes the results of the normative method as inputs and leads indirectly to the results of that normative method being achieved by itself directly resulting in whatever structure of processes and events has these results. Its working can roughly be described as follows: whatever results are described by the normative method of table-laying etiquette, that structure of activity which leads to those results should happen.[3] A result of the normative method of table-laying etiquette might be that the small knife should be to the right of the big knife. The process I am considering has as its result the action that itself leads to the small knife being to the right of the big one. The direct result of this process is not that the knives are in that position, but that the complex process of moving the hand in such a way that the small knife gets put in that position is happening.

Second, there are the processes and events which belong to that structure of activity which results from this first normative process. The action of moving the hand in a certain way would count as belonging to this second category of activity. How such processes work does not really matter for present purposes, except that they happen to lead to the normatively justified results.

Putting these two together gives us a third sort of process: this is the overall process resulting in the normatively justified results. It results in the small knife being positioned to the right of the big knife, and is sensitive to the fact that that is the normatively recommended result. The results of this process *are* described by the normative method. So the normative method does double up as a descriptive method after all. The method will still count as normative, however, and not merely descriptive because it is independent of the second-stage activity which results in the phenomena it justifies. The method of table-laying etiquette is independent of how the process of picking up and moving a knife works.

This means that the description of what is going on in a practically constrained process governed by a normative method can be broken down into two stages. The first stage determines descriptions of results according to the normative method. The second stage establishes descriptions of whatever activity from some repertoire of basic activity leads to those results. The first stage establishes the results to be achieved; the second stage establishes a way of achieving them.

In Chapter 3, Section C, I argued that a means is a practically available part of a causally integrated structure of processes and events which results in the end. This is just what is required to make sense of the two-stage process governed by a normative method.

---

[3] Complications to this description are discussed in the next section.

Whenever a process is governed by a normative method, and the normative method makes recommendations which are not directly available results of that process, the description of the process must have two stages—the normative stage determining the ends and the means-end stage determining the means. If a process is governed by table-laying etiquette, then that process will not only produce the ends recommended by table-laying etiquette, but will also produce the means to those ends—the picking up and moving of knives, etc.

I have been stressing the distinction between a *normative method* whose results are inputs to a process (it governs the process) and a merely *descriptive method* whose results describe the results of a process. What I have shown so far is that when a normative method governs a (practically constrained) process, that process can be described by a descriptive method embodying means-end sensitivity as well as embodying the normative method. This larger method is not itself necessarily a normative method governing that process. And until it is itself a normative method governing a process, then it cannot really be described as a method of practical *justification* for that process. The method describing table-laying means as well as the table-laying ends determined by the rules of etiquette is not itself automatically a normative method governing any process, since it is merely a descriptive method. Only when the means-end considerations are brought from a method describing the overall process into a normative method whose identity is independent of the process, and so may *govern* the process, does it become a method of practical justification.

I am not quite sure what determines this expansion of the normative method governing a process. Perhaps, there is a principle that when a process is governed by a normative method that normative method should generate as complete a description as possible. In that case, when the description about how the process governed by a normative method becomes available, that description must be incorporated into that normative method, which will adapt accordingly. The overall method will still be normative, in virtue of the normativity of the initial method.

There are several different ways that practical justification might be thought to involve means-end justification. It might be that what makes something practically justified is that it is a means to an end. If this were so, then the final end would not itself be practically justified. It would also follow that all practical justification was instrumental. The problem with this is that it is plausible that moral reasoning is concerned with things other than means-end deliberation, yet since moral reasoning tells you what you should do, it is natural to think that it yields descriptions of what is practically justified.

For example, there is one sort of practical justification, according to which you should do such-and-such because that is what some structure of rules (like the rules of table-laying etiquette) says you should do. According to another sort of practical justification, you should do such-and-such because doing that is part of what it is to be a certain kind of person. Although one might use the language of means and ends to describe these kinds of practical justification, the word 'means' would have to be used in quite an extended sense.

There are other ways that practical justification might be thought to involve means-end justification. It might be that what makes something practically justified is that it is an end and that there are means to it. If this were so, then the basic means would not itself be practically justified. This would be a strange restriction on the scope of practical justification.

My position is not committed to either of these two extremes. One can have a notion of practical justification according to which both final ends and basic means are justified. A normative method becomes a method of practical justification when a process which characteristically results in whatever is justified by that method cannot *directly* produce those results. In producing those results it must also produce the means to those results and so ends up producing whatever is justified by a larger method—one based on the original method, but which also incorporates means-end analysis. When this larger method is brought into the normative method which *governs* a process, the normative method becomes a method of practical justification.

It is interesting to contrast this with theoretical justification. Assume for the sake of argument that theoretical justification is justification of beliefs. A normative method incorporating norms of theoretical rationality justifies that a person should have a certain belief. If there is a process which results in what should happen according to this method, it can usually do it directly. A process which is sensitive to the norms of theoretical rationality does not also have to be sensitive to means-end considerations; the formation of beliefs is basic activity for such a process. This is why theoretical justification does not count as a type of practical justification.

This account of means-end justification shows what is wrong with the supposed counter-examples that Woodfield (1976) tries to bring to bear against Charles Taylor's account of teleological explanation (1964). Woodfield considers the example of a U-shaped tube containing water: 'When water is poured down an arm of a U-shaped tube, the level of water in the other arm goes up, because that keeps the levels equal in both arms' (1976: 83). The level goes up because its going up is required for the equalization of the levels. For Taylor, an event is a means to an end if that event is *required* for that end. So, Taylor's condition is satisfied; and then, according to his analysis, it should follow that the water level rises in order to equalize the levels in the two arms. This is indeed the sort of thing we might say. But it is not the sort of thing we should say seriously if we want teleological explanation by itself to capture some notion of purposive agency.

I think that if we look at this example carefully, we can see that it is not true that the water level rises because that is a means to the equalization of the levels. The theoretical method that says that the levels should be kept equal describes a process which directly has this result. There *is* no process resulting in other activity which results in the levels being equal. The level of water in the second arm going up *is* a process which results in the water levels being equal. But this process is the overall process—there are not two stages here. The underlying nature and characteristic stages of the water-level-rising process and of the equalization-of-levels process are identical. They are the same process.

It is for this reason that it is wrong to describe the rising of water in the second arm as happening because it is a means to the equalization of levels. For this to be right there would have to be some second-order process resulting in the water-level-rising process, and this second-order process should generally result in whatever available activity leads to the equalization of levels. There is no such second-order process.

Woodfield has a more general objection, which he calls the double-edge objection: 'Every event brought about in a lawful way occurs because by doing so it accords with the law' (1976: 84). Exactly the same analysis explains why this is not a case of means-end explanation either. Bringing about an event in a lawful way is not the result of a process which leads to whatever activity results in the law being accorded with.

D. SITUATIONAL APPRECIATION

Given a mismatch between the results of a normative method and the activity which is *directly* available to a process, the only way a process can be sensitive to what it should produce according to that normative method is by being sensitive to a larger theoretical method embodying means-end analysis as well. This larger method, when it is itself treated as a normative method, is a method of practical justification. This story needs to be complicated immediately, since means-end analysis may fail to give any description in some cases, and in others it may give several. In either case, the original normative method cannot be expanded into a theoretical method embodying means-ends analysis without some changes.

A normative method may come up with a result which cannot be achieved by any means available to the process. Similarly, since a normative method of some complexity is likely to yield simultaneously several different goal specifications, it may turn out to be impossible to find any means to satisfy the different goals simultaneously. The overall method of justification fails in such cases, since it yields the description that the end will occur while the means-end part of it yields the description that the end will not occur.

One thing that might be done about this is to adapt one's conception of means-end reasoning so that what is described by such reasoning is a set of possible means which satisfies a maximal set of the goals. But this is not very satisfactory. This way of construing the means-end relation is rather arbitrary. Moreover, there is no guarantee that the notion of a maximal set of goals makes sense, for it may not be the case that all the goal specifications are in the same category as far as quantifying is concerned.

Another way to get a coherent overall method would be to insist that the normative method specifies goals in such a way that they can be quantified and compared; so the normative method should specify weightings for the goals that it specifies. This is equivalent to insisting that a normative method should only specify one goal, namely the goal of maximizing the weighted aggregate of all the sub-goals. This is the basis of decision theory. The problem with this is that it forces on us a very limited conception of what can count as a normative method.

What seems to me to be a more satisfactory way to ensure that a normative method can be the basis of a coherent method of practical justification is to have a higher-order method responsible for adapting normative methods in the light of means-end deliberation. The overall method would then yield descriptions of means via a process of looping back and forth from the normative method to means-end deliberation, adapting the normative method in the light of the practicalities until some normative method is arrived at which means-end analysis can be applied to to yield a coherent description of what means should happen.

Wiggins (in Raz 1978: 145) argues that Aristotle has this conception of practical reasoning:

Deliberation is still *zetesis*, a search, but it is not primarily, or at the point of difficulty, a search for means. It is a search for the *best specification* of what would honour or answer to the relevant concerns. Till the specification is available there is no room for the question of means. When this specification is reached, means-end deliberation can start, but difficulties which turn up in this means-end deliberation may send me back a finite number of times to the problem of a better or more practicable specification of the end.

Wiggins suggests that the search for the best specification of the ends requires 'situational appreciation'—this is his interpretation of Aristotle's *aisthesis*. It cannot just be the application of some specifiable set of rules. This is partly because the search involves feedback from means-end deliberation; it involves *seeing what is possible*. Even if the normative method that is arrived at at the end of the process of adaptation is finitely specifiable (and there seems no reason to assume that this is usually going to be the case), that that is the appropriate normative method to apply in that situation requires appreciation of the practical dimensions of the situation.

What are we to say about the possibility that given any particular normative method there may be several different ways to achieve the ends? This possibility arises, however, restrictive we make the repertoire of possible activity. This is the reverse of the problem just considered which was that there might be no way to achieve all the ends. One thing we might say is that practical justification works according to what Kenny (1975) calls the logic of satisfactoriness rather than the logic of satisfaction. The thought here is that several incompatible means may be satisfactory ways to achieve some end; a method of practical justification need not choose from among them, but may make each one of them practically justified. (It is a feature of the logic of satisfactoriness that it does not follow from each one being practically justified that they are all together practically justified.)

So, according to this very natural conception of practical justification, something is practically justified if it is *a* way of achieving the end; it does not have to be the only way. Unfortunately, this natural conception seems to be at odds with my treatment of justification and explanation. I defined a method of justification as a way of deriving a description; not as a way of deriving several alternative descriptions. For this method, when it underlies a causal explanation, must describe a process which *determines* the result.

According to the logic of satisfactoriness, a precisely specified piece of activity might be justified while another incompatible, precisely specified piece of activity is equally practically justified. The problem with this is that we cannot explain why one of these precisely specified pieces of activity happens in terms of its being practically justified. For we cannot explain why that piece of activity rather than the other one happens. All that can be explained is why some less precise (possibly disjunctive) specification of what happens is realized. A method of justification which at a certain level of specificity describes several alternative outcomes cannot properly describe a process which at the same level of specificity results in only one of these outcomes.

If a method of practical justification is to be used to *explain* why a particular result happens, it must specify that particular result and not just a set of results including that one. This means that we must find a way for a method of practical justification to recommend only one result even when there are several means available to achieve some recommended end.

First of all we could extend the conception of a method of practical justification so that the normative method assesses the means as well as the ends. This is a natural extension of the thought that an overall method of practical justification may set up an interplay between normative methods and means-end deliberation.

What is important about this extension to that interplay is that it can allow the construction of a *determinate* method of practical justification out of normative methods and means-end deliberation where no such method was available otherwise.

However, allowing assessment of means as well as of ends does not guarantee that a unique means can be found. It is always going to be a possibility that several equally well-justified ways of reaching an end can be found. As far as the method of justification is concerned, there is nothing to choose between these ways; yet as a matter of practical necessity, one of them must be chosen. This problem is exemplified by Buridan's ass with one pile of hay to the right and one to the left and no reason to choose between them. The ass must then choose at random or make no choice at all.

Buridan's ass may have some unreasoned preference for one of the piles of hay, and this unreasoned preference is why it picks it. In this case, this preference could be incorporated into a determinate method of practical justification. According to this method describing such an ass's behaviour, if there were no objective way to distinguish alternative means then you should adopt whichever one you feel like adopting.

Suppose, however, that Buridan's ass can discern no preference at all. Does this mean that there is absolutely no reason to prefer one means rather than another? There are two ways to ensure a determinate answer from one's method of practical justification for such cases. One way would be to include as part of the method that in genuine Buridan's-ass cases a choice should be made at random. The other way would be to base the choice on the first means you think of. In either case a reason has been *constructed* for acting one way rather than another. A method is being employed which recommends a particular result. The method responds to arbitrary factors, the result of a coin-toss, for instance, but such factors are still reasons despite being arbitrary.

Another way of resolving the problem would be to allow the method of practical justification to come up with descriptions of a less specific sort. It may be that there is no method at all operating in the ass which justifies one choice rather than the other, not even one which responds to arbitrary factors. Perhaps, what is practically justified for the ass is that it either eats the left-hand pile of hay or it eats the right-hand pile of hay. According to this method, it is not practically justified for the ass to eat one rather than the other pile. That it goes on to eat one rather than the other pile is then not to be explained teleologically, since the teleological explanation stops at the disjunction.

E. ESTABLISHING THE FACTS

Another factor that complicates the structure of means-end justification is information. An exactly similar move can be made with respect to informational means as was made in Section C with respect to practical means. In Section C, I argued that, unless a normative method is very limited or unless the process which is supposed to result in what is justified has an unlimited repertoire of basic activity, then the process will need to establish means in order to establish the ends specified by the normative method. So, associated with the normative method will be a larger method also incorporating means-end sensitivity.

Similarly, unless a normative method is very limited—limited to an area governed by established facts—or unless the relevant process has an unlimited repertoire of facts at its disposal, then the process will need to establish some facts before determining the appropriate means. So, associated with the method of practical justification, there will be a larger method also incorporating sensitivity to what are the informational means to establishing what are the practical means to the ends specified by the normative method. For example, if the end is to have a bottle of beer, the informational means might include finding out whether there is one in the fridge, while the practical means will be to take one out of the fridge, open it, etc.

A fairly standard way to understand the notion of establishing a fact is in terms of forming a true belief in a certain kind of way. The difference between epistemological internalism and epistemological externalism is a difference in how to spell out the certain kind of way that constrains how a true belief should be formed if it is to count as the *establishment* of a fact. According to internalism, there are internal requirements on how the belief should be formed—in terms of its logical relationship with other beliefs and appearances. According to externalism, the requirements are external—perhaps in terms of the reliability of the way the belief is formed.

But for my purposes, even this form of epistemological externalism is too internalist. I want to explicate the notion of establishing a fact without referring to beliefs at all, but instead by considering the progression of a teleological process.

Consider a teleological process governed by a method of practical justification which as yet has no sensitivity to informational means. Suppose that the method recommends the end that I drink a bottle of beer and goes on to recommend as the means to that end that I take a bottle of beer out of the fridge, etc. The process governed by this method will not work properly until I have found out where to locate a bottle of beer. But the activity of finding out where to locate a bottle of beer is not itself recommended by the method; being able to understand the notion of establishing a fact forms no part of knowing such a primitive method of practical justification. So we can make sense of the idea of a process being governed by a method of practical justification without exploiting the notion of establishing a fact.

This means that it should be possible to explicate the notion of establishing a fact in terms of the working of such a process. What it means to say that the fact that there is a beer in the fridge has been established is to say that, to the extent that this fact determines or might determine what should happen according to some method of practical justification, the teleological mechanism governed by that method of practical justification does or would have the corresponding results. What it is to have established that there is a beer in the fridge is to be in a position not to need to open the door and peer inside before acting rationally with respect to this fact.

Just because I have established that there is a beer in the fridge, it does not mean that all behaviour which is justified due to this fact will occur instantly; I may need to establish various other facts too—like where is the bottle-opener. What it does mean is that *to the extent that* the answer to the question of whether there is a beer in the fridge is relevant to what should happen, the teleological mechanism governing my behaviour will work properly. Now, even when I have not established whether there is a beer in the fridge, the teleological mechanism governing my behaviour *may* work properly with respect to the question of how to get myself a beer, since it may result in my taking a look in the fridge, and then picking out a beer. The point is that until I have established whether there is a beer in the fridge there will be *some* potential situations where my teleological mechanism will not work properly. For example, if I needed to say instantly where there was certainly a beer I would not be able to. So a teleological mechanism has established a fact if for *any* potential situation where that fact determines what should happen according to the method of practical justification governing the way that mechanism works, the mechanism will work properly.

Suppose that I am staring gloomily out of the window at the rain. According to my account, I have established that it is raining even though I do nothing that uses the fact. I have established that it is raining in virtue of the fact that *if* the justification of some action depended on this fact (for example, if I had the goal of getting wet straightaway), and I had established all the other relevant facts, then the action would follow. So establishing a fact can be done independently of any *manifested* advance in one's rational achievement of goals. But there must be an advance that is at least *manifestable*.

There are means to establishing facts just as there are means to achieving practical goals. The means are built up out of basic fact-establishing activity and other activity. In the case of establishing whether there is a beer in the fridge, the means was opening the fridge door, peering inside, and looking to see if there is a beer there. The looking to see is basic activity; it itself does not have a means, but is part of the repertoire of activity directly available to the method describing my behaviour.

Such basic perceptual activity can be characterized in terms of establishing the facts, and so can be specified by reference to making potential progress with teleological processes rather than by reference to mental states. I think that looking to see if something is there in front of me may be understood as something like establishing whether or not a recognizable object is in my line of view. This is itself to be understood as one's teleological mechanism advancing with respect to the question of whether some recognizable object is there in one's direct line of view. This is activity that a method governing my behaviour can regard as directly available (though, of course, it could not if I were blind).

I think that using this notion of establishing the facts is the right way to approach questions concerning the nature of perception and of knowledge. But I do not need to defend that claim here. Even if looking and seeing involve more than just making potential advances in teleological processes, it is this notion of making potential advances in teleological processes that is needed in an account of informational means.

Just as there are perceptual means to establishing facts, so there are intellectual means to establishing facts. For example, instead of establishing that there is a beer in the fridge by looking, I might establish the same fact by thinking about it. I might remember how many beers I bought, how many were in the fridge before, how many I have drunk since, and calculate how many remain.

One might think that in some sense the fact was already established; I did not have to do anything active before my teleological process could progress with regard to this fact. But the point is that this teleological process cannot produce its results *right away* before the fact has been established. Sometimes remembering, inferring, calculating, etc. take some time, and then some identifiable progress is made by teleological processes when these activities occur. Suppose that it takes a few seconds to remember how many bottles of beer I bought. Then, before these few seconds, had I needed to act instantly in a way that depended on this fact, I would not have been able to. For example, if I had had to answer truthfully and instantly, I would not have been able to. After the activity of remembering, I would have been able to answer truthfully and instantly. Progressing from the state where I could not answer truthfully and instantly to one where I could, counts as establishing a fact.

Even when remembering, inferring, etc. take no more time than it takes to answer a question, they might count as making some teleological progress. Suppose that bringing some fact to mind takes no time at all. There might still be parts of a teleological process that would take some time to produce a result that depended on that fact which after that fact was brought to mind would take no time at all. For example, suppose that I know perfectly well that there is a bottle of beer in the fridge; if asked whether there is a bottle of beer in the fridge I will be able to answer instantly. However, it may be the case that when the need for a bottle of beer arises I do not think immediately of the one in the fridge. Now, if I have just brought to mind the fact that there is a bottle of beer in the fridge, then I will be able to act instantly to satisfy the need. So, bringing to mind a fact in such circumstances, even though it takes no time to do, still counts as establishing a fact, according to my account.

Establishing a fact that has been established before, given certain conditions about how long ago the fact was established and whether it has been put to any use since, counts as basic activity that is directly available for a method describing my behaviour. It is my contention that it is this sort of establishing of facts, when it is basic, that constitutes *remembering*. (When it is not basic, but is done through other means—e.g. perceptual means—it is not to be counted as remembering.) But as with the parallel claim made about perception, I do not need to defend the contention here.

Similarly, when a set of facts has been established, establishing simple inferences from this set counts as basic activity that is available for the method describing my behaviour. The structure consisting of establishing how many beers I bought, establishing how many beers were already in the fridge, establishing how many beers I drank, and establishing the total number of remaining beers after making the addition and subtraction is a means to establishing how many beers there are in the fridge.

Whenever a process is governed by a method of practical justification, that process will in fact be described by a larger theoretical method which is sensitive to whether relevant facts have yet been established and what are the informational means to establishing these facts. This larger theoretical method embodying these informational considerations may then be brought into the method of practical justification. This is exactly parallel to the earlier stage where a process governed by a normative method is seen to be sensitive to considerations of practical means; when these considerations are incorporated into the normative method, it becomes a method of practical justification. This progression of a normative method into a method incorporating practical means and then into one incorporating informational means looks quite similar to the progression of Hegelian dialectic discussed in Chapter 1. What seems to drive the progression is something like self-consciousness. A process which results in what should happen according to some method of justification works in a certain way which is not yet part of that method. These extra considerations are then brought into the method of justification—this is the stage we might describe as self-consciousness. The method of justification must then adapt to accommodate these new considerations.

Wiggins's notion of situational appreciation can then be extended to include informational appreciation. We have seen that through the higher-order method of situational appreciation, the normative method that is to be employed in a method of practical justification is partly determined by practical considerations concerning the availability of means. Similarly, the normative method will be partly determined by informational considerations concerning the availability of ways of discovering the means. If there is no way that I could discover where to find a bottle of beer I should change my goal.

A process which is governed by such a method of practical justification will also involve higher-order establishing of facts. It will have to establish what is the informational means to establishing some answer. For example, if I have not yet established that the fridge is a plausible place to find beers, then I may need to establish what is a good way to look for beers even before I establish where there is a beer. There will be a set of constraints that operate here too. The informational means may itself be available, while there is no available way to establish what it is. These constraints may then be brought into the normative method themselves; and so it goes on. There is no danger of an infinite regress here. A method of practical justification will only incorporate informational sensitivity to a certain level; what enables a process to be governed by such a method despite this is that part of the activity of the process will be undirected exploratory behaviour which is not specifically justified by the method.

One final refinement to the notion of establishing a fact should be considered. Suppose that I find myself unable to bring to mind what someone's name is when required to introduce them, though I would have no trouble in saying for any candidate name whether or not it was theirs. In one sense I can remember their name; in another I cannot. This makes it difficult to know whether to say that the fact that their name is, say, Julie is established. There is a distinction here which the broad notion of establishing a fact ignores.

The key point here is that, strictly speaking, a teleological process makes progress, not with regard to facts, but with regard to questions. What are really established are not facts but answers. So, for a teleological process to have an answer to question, Q, established is for it to have progressed so that in any situation where the recommended activity depends on what is the answer to Q, this recommended activity will occur. In the situation just described, my teleological process has progressed with respect to the question: 'Is this person's name Julie?' but not with respect to the question: 'What is this person's name?' Having made this distinction, I will not be very rigorous about it since the improvement in precision would be outweighed by the increase in complication. For example, if I wanted to make my account of beliefs in the next chapter properly rigorous, it would have to be ramified in line with this distinction.

F. SUBJECTIVITY

The considerations of the previous sections go some way towards recognizing the subjective nature of practical justification. What basic activity can be produced varies from subject to subject. If a method of practical justification is to determine the workings of an actual subject it should work with a particular repertoire of basic activity. If I only had one arm, a method of practical justification which recommends that I should clasp my hands together will have no chance of governing the process resulting in my behaviour. In fact, even this repertoire of basic activity is open to adaptation by the higher-order method looping between the normative method and the means-end deliberation. For a subject's repertoire of basic activity can be enhanced.

Similarly, the sort of information-gathering activity that counts as directly available varies from subject to subject. The method of practical justification governing a subject's activity, as it becomes more inclusive, will take this into account. In this way, the method of practical justification that governs a subject's activity becomes tailored for the subject. The question of this section is what sort of information should we say that such a method employs. Will such a method employ all facts, just the available facts, just the established facts, or perhaps not facts at all, but beliefs?

Consider first a method of practical justification which does not involve sensitivity to informational means. There is no problem with having the information which is used by such a method to consist of all facts, whether knowable or not. The process which is determined by this method will not work when the relevant facts are not available to the process. This can be put down to a failure in the activation conditions of the underlying mechanism. The activation conditions will include some condition like that the relevant facts are available.

This move is not available when we go on to consider more sophisticated methods of practical justification which do involve sensitivity to informational means. Such methods would issue contradictory descriptions in situations where the relevant information is not available. On the one hand, the methods would recommend the unknowable means to the end. On the other hand, they might recommend, for example, that if the information concerning how to achieve one goal is not available, the goal should be changed.

So, for such sophisticated methods of practical justification to be coherent, they must work with a different conception of the facts—a more subjective conception. Consider first the slightly less objective conception of facts which the method could use, namely that of the *establishable* facts. This conception does not go far enough. The degree to which it is justified for the system to discover facts depends on the situation—discovering all establishable facts is not a practical possibility (though of course for each establishable fact, discovering it is a practical possibility). There will be situations where the method recommends not bothering to establish the required facts since the search would be too costly, but changing the goal instead. If this method employed the establishable facts it would also recommend achieving the goal by establishable means. So, with this conception of the available facts, such a method is incoherent.

More promising would be a conception of the facts as the facts which *should be* established according to the method. But this is still not quite subjective enough a conception. The subject will always be able to establish facts that no method can say it should establish. For example, something may be noticed by pure chance. A subject may (perhaps through the recommendation of the method) indulge in undirected exploratory behaviour. What facts are established through such behaviour cannot be determined by any conception of facts that *should be* established. Conversely, a subject may fail to have established facts that should be established. If the method of justification governing the subject's activity is inclusive enough to be sensitive to what facts the subject has established, then it had better not employ those facts which the subject should establish. Where there is a mismatch between what the subject should have established and what it has established, the method will yield contradictory descriptions.

So the information that is to be employed by a reasonably inclusive method of practical justification governing some process had better consist of those facts that *are established* by that process. This restriction ensures that the information used by a method is sufficiently subjective that the method is fit to govern the activity of a self-conscious subject. But now, someone might worry that this restriction, by incorporating some degree of subjectivity, has threatened the externalism of my account.

It is important to remain clear that the inputs to such a method are still facts about the world; they are not (though they might include) facts about the subject. There is a distinction between restricting the inputs to be employed by a method of practical justification to the facts established by the subject and restricting the inputs to facts about what is established by the subject. The reasons that emerge from a method restricted in the first way are still predominantly externalist not internalist, although there will be internalist reasons too.

But the worry might remain that, although teleological reasons are externalist according to this account, the account itself must employ reference to mental states. If this were the case, then the account I am trying to provide of what constitutes intentional action could not be adapted to be an account of mental states. Teleological Behaviourism would be undermined.

Establishing the facts is certainly a mental notion. But I think it is possible to give an account of it in terms of making progress with teleological processes. So, if this account works, there need be no reference to mental states in the account of practical justification. There is still a risk of circularity, however. The teleological processes, progress in which defines establishing the facts, are teleological in virtue of being governed by a method of practical justification. If an account of that method of practical justification requires the facts employed by that method to be established by the teleological process then the circularity is in place.

However, according to the way I have set up the account, there is no circle, only a spiral. My account can be seen as a way of building up to a notion of agency in steps. The unsophisticated method of practical justification that does not involve self-consciousness about informational availability can work with a baldly externalist conception of the facts. We can get a handle on the notions of agency and of establishing facts from consideration of how a process determined by such a method works. Then, the notions developed at this stage can be applied to the next stage to give a more subjective conception of practical justification. Eventually we can allow methods of practical justification to involve consideration of the subject's own mental states. The account of what it is for the subject to have these mental states is provided by looking at methods of practical justification at earlier stages of the progression—methods which do not involve considerations of such things.

Against all this, an internalist about practical justification would argue that the means to an end in a method of practical justification should not be determined by the facts at all, but by the beliefs, whether they are true or not. But this internalist position suffers from the problem that the method does not describe the means to ends but only the apparent means to ends. When some relevant belief is false, a process governed by such an internalist method will not result in the desired end at all. This is despite the fact that it works rationally according to the method. Whether or not the process does lead to the desired end depends on factors completely outside of the internalist mechanism. I think that this means that for a radically internalist method to be coherent, the ends that it justifies can only be *attempts* to achieve objective results.[4] But in that case, there is not the separation between the means and the end—according to this method, between the apparent means and the attempt to achieve the end—that is characteristic of practical justification.

This seems surprising for philosophers brought up with the following internalist schema for practical justification:

I1. *S* believes that *P* is the means to *Q*.
S wants *Q*.
So, *S* should achieve *P*.

As it stands, this might count as part of a method of practical justification even according to my characterization. For the whole schema might be taken to be a normative method embedded in a larger method embodying genuine means-end rationality. The

---

[4] I tried to show this in Chapter 1, Section C.

schema provides an end; the genuine means-end stage occurs in finding a way to achieve that end. For example, it might be that R is the actual means to achieve P given the repertoire of basic activity available to S. Then the larger method of practical justification would recommend that R happens. Of course, this move means that the overall method of practical justification ceases to be internalist at all. It also means that the schema is just one among many initially acceptable normative methods.

The question of the propriety of purely internalist methods of practical justification can be made sharper if we ask whether the schema counts as a method of practical justification all by itself. Would it be a method of practical justification if P were included in the repertoire of basic activity that goes with the method, and required no other activity in order to be achieved? The general question is whether a method which takes us from mental states to results by itself may count as a method of practical justification.

Let me start by considering an even simpler internalist schema:

I2. I want Q.
So, Q should happen.

Q should be thought of as something like: 'That my eyes blink now'. Whereas this looks like a perfectly good, though extremely selfish, normative method, it is hard to see what makes it constitute a method of practical justification. It is certainly not a universally sound practical schema. A Buddhist alternative would be the following:

I3. I want Q.
So, I should stop wanting Q.

According to this alternative schema, it is not rational for Q to be achieved just because the subject wants it. This kind of exception might be eliminated if we substitute 'intend' for 'want'. I do not think that this substitution eliminates all such exceptions. But, to the extent that it does, this is due to the collapse of any interesting separation between the mental state and the thing that it is justifying. This collapse stops the method from being a normative method at all.

The original schema, I1, can be divided into two parts. I2, or something like it, takes us from the want to the achievement of the want. The other part is the bit involving the apparent means-end rationality. So, perhaps it is this that is supposed to make the schema one of practical justification. This other part is the following:

14. *S* believes that *P* is the means to *Q*.
    S wants *Q*.
    So, *S* wants *P*.

This schema takes one from mental states to mental state, and in this respect is like theoretical justification of belief in terms of other beliefs. What is supposed to make it practical is that wanting (or intending) leads naturally to action and the attempted achievement of the want (or intention). It is a schema which justifies practically orientated mental states in terms of other mental states. This sort of schema seems to me to have the best chance of any internalist schema to count by itself as a method of practical justification.

I think that if we ever had such an internalist method of practical justification, it would get rejected in the course of self-conscious consideration. Such justifications are not very good justifications. When a belief is rational, albeit false, then it may justify desires and actions in some sense. But this may be because, in order for the belief to be rational, there must be some relevant facts behind the belief, and these make the desires and actions objectively justified in some sense. But now, if internalist practical rationality *did* justify such things, then even totally (objectively) irrational beliefs would justify them.

Suppose I believe that my car is parked in Street A. Suppose this is just some mental confusion and I really parked it in Street B but have temporarily forgotten. Is my action of walking up and down Street A justified by this belief?

I suggest that if one is inclined to answer yes to this question, one is forced to justify the answer by finding some objective facts to do the real justifying work. For example, perhaps I usually leave the car on Street A, so it is a good bet that I will do so on this occasion. But if this was the justification, then the belief is not relevant; the objective fact is doing the work.

Suppose I have never parked on Street A in my life and that the psychological reason for my belief is that I have been listening to someone talking about Street A. One is less inclined to say that my behaviour is justified. However, in even the most apparently irrational behaviour we can find some objective justification. In this case, there is an objective fact, which is that Street A has some significance for me. So on this basis there is some objective justification for believing that I parked the car there.

Even without any such flimsy justification for the belief, the action may be objectively justified given the belief. It is an objective fact that my unthinking beliefs usually turn out right; so it is a good bet to act on this one. Note that it is not the belief that has any intrinsic justifying role here. If I was prone to getting voices in my ear saying, 'You have parked in Street X,' and they usually turned out right, then it would be rational to go to Street X whether or not I had any beliefs about it.

If someone's unreasoned beliefs were generally a bad indicator of the way the world was, then that person would not be justified in following them. Some theories of belief rule out the possibility of entirely irrational beliefs that are entirely unreliable (e.g. Dretske 1988). According to such theories, a belief is essentially a reliable indicator of the world. So beliefs will always justify action. But, of course, these theories accept that the justifying work is done by the objective facts underpinning the beliefs.

If my analysis is right, the obvious question is why is there such a powerful intuition in favour of some internalist schema characterizing a method of practical justification. I suggest in answer to this that subjective reasons provide *excuses* rather than real justifications. They only justify in the sense of mitigate. The basis for this suggestion is in the distinction between a reason *meaning* it is rational for P to happen and a reason *making* it rational for P to happen. Truly justificatory reasons make what they justify rational. Mitigatory reasons only show what they justify to be rational.

Intending to eat means that it is rational to eat, but it does not make it rational. Believing that the food is poisonous means that it is rational not to eat, but it does not make it rational. What makes it rational is the *fact* that the food is poisonous or the fact that the evidence suggests that the food is poisonous. I think that the same applies to internalist theoretical justification. Believing the food to be poisonous means that it is rational to believe that I will be unwell if I eat it. But again, it does not make this belief rational. What makes the belief rational are the facts on which the belief is based.

If you have the appropriate belief–desire pair, it *follows* that it is practically justified for you to achieve or at any rate attempt to achieve the apparent means. But achieving or attempting to achieve the apparent means is not practically justified *in virtue* of the belief–desire pair. The presence of the belief–desire pair merely shows that there is something which makes the activity practically justified.

A claim that I will be making in the final chapter is that intentional mental states should be attributed in virtue of the presence of mechanisms which work according to a scheme of practical justification of the externalist sort that I have been working out in this chapter. It will be possible to use this claim about the attribution of beliefs and intentions to show that whenever it is right to attribute the belief that *P* is the best means to *Q* and to attribute the intention to achieve *Q*, there is a scheme of practical justification operating for the agent according to which it is rational to achieve *P*.

To make this work, there is one further adaptation to the notion of practical justification that I will have to make. I want to explain a conception of practical justification according to which activity involving *false* beliefs can still be practically justified. This activity may fail to achieve its goal and yet still be practically justified. I want to show how this is possible even within an externalist conception of practical justification. This is the task of the next section.

G. WORKING ASSUMPTIONS

Suppose that I misremember how to wire up an electric plug properly, and attach the blue wire to the live terminal. In one respect there is a failure of rationality here. But in another respect the behaviour is justified. According to the Teleological Theory of Action, the behaviour does not constitute an action unless it is justified, and there seems to be no doubt that the behaviour does constitute an action in this case. According to an internalist conception of practical justification, this behaviour is justified in terms of the belief that the blue wire is connected to the live terminal when the plug is wired up properly and the desire to wire up the plug properly. But, on the face of it, according to an externalist conception of practical justification which works only with facts, the behaviour is not justified.

I want to suggest a way to complicate the notion of a method of practical justification still further in order to accommodate this sort of situation while not compromising the externalist nature of the method. Let me start with the notion of a method of practical justification already restricted by some conception of what sort of facts are available to it. Only those facts which are established should be used. The extra restriction I propose is to take some proposition, *P*, and require that the method should work on the assumption that *P* is true unless some further information contradicting *P* becomes established. It should work on this assumption whether or not it has established that *P*. In addition to working with the established facts as inputs, the method has a working assumption *embedded* in it.

For example, *P* might be the proposition that the correct way to wire up a plug is to attach the blue wire to the live terminal. Having this as a working assumption in a method of practical justification which has wiring up a plug properly as an end will lead to the conclusion that the appropriate means is that the blue wire should be attached to the live terminal. The embedded assumption also may affect what ends are recommended by the method, either directly or through some process of situational appreciation. If it is impossible to attach the blue wire to the live terminal, then some other goal may be recommended as a result.

If facts concerning the correct way to wire up a plug become established, these facts will trump the working assumption and the method will have to adapt. The method will not recommend actively seeking out such facts, since the method can quite happily work on an assumption concerning them. But when such a fact is established even given that—e.g. the electrician gives me an unsolicited lesson on the right way to do it—the working assumption lapses. So false working assumptions are naturally unstable.

Given the view of a normative method that I am recommending in Section B, we can think of a method embedding a working assumption at one time and then the *same* method adapting in the light of further information becoming rationally available, and then no longer embedding that assumption (or embedding a contrary assumption). So we can think of a single teleological mechanism governed by such an evolving method at one time resulting in attaching the blue wire to the live terminal and then resulting in attaching it to the neutral terminal after the false working assumption has lapsed.

The refinement made at the end of Section E suggests that the more precise notion would be that of a working *answer* rather than a working assumption. We would say that a method works with *P* as a working answer to the question, Q, if and only if whenever a situation arises where the answer to Q makes a difference to what is recommended by that method, the method works on the assumption that the answer is P, whether or not this is something which has been established by the process governed by the method. However, for simplicity, I am going to continue to talk about working assumptions for the time being.

Working assumptions do not have to be limited to information relevant to what is the best means to some end. A method might equally well embody the working assumption that some end, E, is to be achieved. As with working assumptions about what is a means to an end, such working assumptions about what ends are to be achieved may lapse in the light of further information. In situations where the established facts combined with the rest of the method contradict this working assumption, the method fails to give a recommendation and must adapt.

When the correct information concerning the working assumption is not established and when the working assumption is false, a process governed by such a restricted method may fail to result in the ends determined by the method. The process no longer characteristically results in what should happen according to the method. This is clearly a problem. It appears that the method is not a method of practical justification after all. As with the radically internalist method, the method does not incorporate genuine means-end deliberation, but only apparent means-end deliberation.

Unlike with the case of the radically internalist method, the problem can be overcome. The problem is overcome if all the working assumptions are isolated in the stage of the overall method of practical justification which determines the ends to be achieved rather than in the stage which determines the means to those ends. This is done by incorporating any part of the original means-end deliberation which exploits the working assumptions into that part of the overall method responsible for determining ends. The method determining the ends to be achieved would no longer yield the recommendation that correct wiring of the plug should be achieved. Instead, it yields the recommendation that whatever would be a means to the correct wiring of the plug *given* the working assumptions should be achieved. The overall method of practical justification will incorporate a stage of genuine means-end deliberation, which determines how these weaker goals recommended by the end-determining part of the method should be achieved.

The overall method still has two stages, one determining ends and another determining means to those ends. Any influence of the working assumptions is isolated in the part determining ends. So the overall method counts as a method of practical justification according to my characterization. My hand moves in a certain way because that is part of the way to attach the blue wire to the live terminal. What we cannot say is that I attach the blue wire to the live terminal because that is the way to wire the plug up properly.

This manœuvre does not work, however, if there is no part of the overall method which is not affected by the working assumptions. In particular, if there is a working assumption concerning the effects of all the basic activity available to the process, then there will be no space for any genuine means-end stage. So the role of working assumptions in a method of practical justification must be restricted to some extent; there must be some facts concerning the effects of basic activity which are not incorporated as working assumptions.

Consider the victims of an evil demon or mad scientist. Whenever they take themselves to be performing some basic activity they are systematically deceived and the activity that does occur has none of the implications that they are looking for. According to my account, it is wrong to count the activity that occurs as practically justified. This seems to be quite a natural restriction. In this example, there may be a way of systematically mapping the activity which does happen on to activity which would be practically justified. It is activity that would be practically justified given the truth of the working assumptions. But this is not enough to make the activity that does happen actually practically justified. There is no appropriate sensitivity in what actually happens to what should happen; so the process is not governed by any conception of practical justification.

This does not disallow a method of practical justification from employing an indefinite number of working assumptions. It would still have two stages, one recommending ends and the other recommending actual means to achieving those ends, as long as the working assumptions did not cover every question of practical means. The sort of thing that is disallowed by this restriction from counting as subject to practical justification is a computer system which has no capacity to learn from experience. All the information used by the normative method governing such a system is fixed in the form of working assumptions. There is no openness to the way the world actually is.

Whenever a process has a fact established, that process is governed by a method of practical justification which takes that established fact as an input. So, the method governing the process works on the assumption that there is such a fact. This is not quite the same thing as saying that the method *embeds* that fact as a working assumption. The difference is that the identity of a method which embeds a proposition as a working assumption is determined by that proposition, whereas the identity of a method which takes the established fact as an input is not.

There is nothing stopping us from taking a fact that has been established by a process and adapting the method governing the process by embedding that fact as a working assumption. This is to take something which was an input to one method and bring it into an adapted version of that method as a fixed point—a sort of axiom. Both methods work on the assumption that that proposition is true. For as long as the fact remains established the two methods give the same recommendations. The second one is more unstable, however, since it lapses if the fact is no longer established. We could even construct a very unstable method which embodies all the facts that are established. But such a method would have no space for genuine means-end reasoning and would not count as a method of practical justification.

5

Agency

A. ACTIONS

According to the Teleological Theory of Action, activity constitutes an action in virtue of being teleologically explainable—it constitutes action if it happens because it should. I am now in a position to tie up the loose ends from Chapter 1, and give some more worked-out version of my theory of action. One question that I want to consider in this section is what 'constitutes' amounts to in this formulation of the theory. What precisely is the relation between this activity which is teleologically explainable and the action that can be identified in virtue of the availability of such an explanation?

First, it is worth reconsidering whether the theory needs to be stated in terms of explanation at all. This stress on explanation in my approach, I think, just reflects its historical context. The ground-breaking work of Anscombe still informs current discussion of action. She characterizes intentional actions as those 'to which a certain sense of the question "Why?" is given application' (1957: 9). But if Chapter 2 is on the right track, then this talk of explanation can be eliminated in exchange for talk of processes and theoretical methods describing processes. Indeed, as I try to show in Chapter 3, Section B, we must make this exchange if we want to give our account a way of ruling out deviant causal chains—where things happen because they should, but in the wrong sort of way.

When my account of causal explanation is applied to the Teleological Theory of Action, we get the following claim:

> Activity constitutes action in virtue of resulting from a process which is governed by a method of practical justification.

What I have tried to show in Chapter 4, Sections A–C is that a method of practical justification must:

(i) be normative
(ii) embody means-end sensitivity.

Condition (i) requires that the method have some identity independent of the process at issue. Although it serves as a description
of the process, it must *govern* the process. The process must result
in whatever the method recommends. If the method came up with
a different result, the process would have to adapt to that, rather
than vice versa. Condition (ii) is what justifies our calling any such
process a *teleological* process.

There may be a worry that this is not a strong-enough condition
for action. So, in Chapter 3, I have tried to show that the activity of
current-day computers, lower organisms, human organs, etc., do
not result from any teleological process. The activity of evolution
may result from a teleological process of some sort, but not one
with a tight-enough conception of teleology. The process of evolution results in that type of activity that bears a certain relation to
activity that would be practically justified. It does not result in that
type of activity that is itself practically justified.

A converse worry is that, given my externalist conception of
practical justification, the Teleological Theory of Action requires
too strong a condition for action. The worry is that no natural
process could be truly teleological. In Chapter 4 I have tried to
show that there is an externalist conception of practical justification
that respects subjectivity and that could truly govern a natural
process, where not every sort of activity was available to the process, nor every sort of information. I hope that by my account of
processes in Chapter 2 I have also alleviated the worry that no
process could be truly teleological because no process could get
things right in every circumstance. I only require a process to get
things right when it is working properly.

The Teleological Theory of Action can be given a more metaphysical slant by being used as the basis of an answer to the
question: what sort of things are actions? Given the distinction
argued for in Chapter 2, Section B, between processes that persist in
time and events which extend over time, the first question is
whether an action is a process or an event (or perhaps something
else again). Consider the example of my brushing my teeth one
evening. It seems that there is both an event and a process to be
identified here. What was happening while I was brushing my teeth

was a process of my brushing my teeth. What happened when I brushed my teeth was an event of my brushing my teeth. The event in this case is the completion of the process. Either can count as an action—the action that was happening and the action that happened. It seems that in this area the distinction between the process and the event consisting of the completion of that process does not have much significance. On my view, the process is the more basic of the two categories. So I will talk about action-*processes* for simplicity, while not meaning to exclude action-*events* consisting of the completions of action-processes.

Given the Teleological Theory of Action, there are two possible theories of the identity of actions that naturally suggest themselves. According to one theory, an action is to be identified with a teleological process; while, according to the other theory, an action is to be identified with the result of a teleological process. The first theory has an attractive simplicity at first glance, but if it is to stand a chance as the basis of the right account, it needs to be made a lot more complicated. For not every teleological process counts as an action. There is an overarching teleological process which is that of living and behaving rationally. This is the process which might be thought to unify a person's life.[1] It is not itself an action. A teleological process which embeds the working assumption that some goal, G, is to be achieved stands a better chance of counting as an action. But such a process might result in all sorts of stage-setting activity that occurs before the action. For example, a teleological process which has as a working assumption that I am to brush my teeth may result in my buying a toothbrush; but this forms no part of my action of brushing my teeth.

It might be possible to think of a way of constraining teleological processes so that they had the right kind of dimensions to count as actions. But this approach is beginning to look *ad hoc*. The approach also has problems at the other end of the spectrum of actions with basic actions like raising one's hand or blinking (when that blinking is intentional). If these pieces of activity are really basic, then they cannot be themselves teleological processes. They do not involve any means-end sensitivity since the end is already a basic means.

Within some piece of basic activity there is still quite a lot of

---

[1] A Teleological Behaviourist's account of personal identity would focus on this process.

unconscious adaptation to the requirements of the situation. Which muscles contract to raise my hand depends on where my hand is situated with respect to my body; how much they have to contract depends on how much resistance there is. If these adaptations were completely unconscious, then they would be like the adaptations of the pancreas to blood-sugar level considered in Chapter 3, Section E. These adaptations do not count as teleological. What makes this case more complicated is that some of these adaptations can be made conscious. To that extent the characterization of this activity as basic comes under pressure. But this flexibility concerning the basicness of such activity cannot really be used to defend the claim that all actions are teleological processes. All we have to do is to find some activity which is unequivocally basic. This cannot count as a teleological process, but is presumably still an action.

There are some further moves that someone defending the theory that an action is a special kind of teleological process might make. But I think that there is a better theory which should be introduced instead. This is that an action is a *result* of a teleological process. Teleological processes result in means and ends being achieved; so this theory identifies actions with the achievements of means and ends.

In Chapter 3, Section C, I defined a means in terms of the notion of available activity. Available activity was defined inductively as either activity from the repertoire of basic activity or a causally integrated structure consisting of pieces of available activity along with other pieces of activity which would happen if the earlier part of the structure happened. A means to an end is defined as a piece of available activity which belongs to a larger piece of available activity which results in the end. The achievement of the end is the larger piece of available activity; a means is a component of this larger structure which is also a piece of available activity.

As an example, consider as an end that my teeth are to be brushed this evening. There are different ways of constructing a causally integrated structure of pieces of activity which results in this end. Consider the following structure: during my lunch-hour I go to the supermarket and buy a toothbrush which I carry with me until I get home; in the evening I take the toothbrush out of its packaging, squeeze some toothpaste onto it, hold it under a tap, turn the tap, let some water fall on to the toothbrush, wetting it, etc. In this structure, the piece of activity which is the water falling from the tap is not itself available activity. All the other pieces are. The water falling from the tap is a piece of activity that will happen if the earlier pieces in the structure happen. So the whole structure is an available piece of activity (although, by itself, the water falling is not available activity). The component pieces are available because they themselves consist of a structure of available pieces of activity and other pieces that will happen if the earlier pieces happen. At the bottom level, the pieces of activity are available because they belong to some repertoire of basic activity that goes to define the particular method of practical justification that is operating here.

This is a very sketchy account, but I think that it must be at least roughly right. A method of practical justification which works with this notion of the means-end relation will recommend of all these pieces of available activity that they occur. If a process is governed by the method of practical justification, then it will be a teleological process and will result in these pieces of available activity. According to the account of action that I am considering, each of these pieces of available activity counts as an action—from the basic activity to the whole structure of activity (which may include pieces of non-available activity) that results in the final end. Some of these actions may themselves be teleological processes of a limited sort. But basic actions like raising one's hand are not teleological processes.

This account implies that all actions are in some sense rational. Given my account of practical rationality in the previous chapter, this does not commit me to the Davidsonian view that all actions are done for a reason which consists of a belief–desire pair. This Davidsonian view is attacked convincingly by Hursthouse (1991). She argues for what she calls arational actions, like jumping for joy or tearing up the photograph of someone one is angry with. I think that the word 'arational' is unfortunate. The reason I jumped was that I was joyful. The reason I tore up the photograph was that I was angry with you. Moreover, even if these actions cannot be explained rationally as emotional responses (which I think they can), they are nevertheless recommended by a method of practical justification, and that is why they happen. The fact that the achievement of a top-level goal is not a means does not stop it from being practically justified, since the method of practical justification incorporates the normative method which determines the top-level goals.

The notion of a means defined in Chapter 3, Section C, was extended in Chapter 4 to include informational means. Given this, my theory of action allows the finding out of some information to count as an action, since it is a result of a teleological process. This inclusion seems quite natural. One of the things you may have to do in order to wire up a plug properly is to find out how to wire up a plug properly. Along with the other things you have to do, like attaching the blue wire to the neutral terminal, this seems to be an intentional action.

This theory of action has implications for the question of when actions begin and end. Consider, for example, Oswald's action of shooting the president. Does this action include the bullet flying through the air and striking the president or does the action end with the last bit of Oswald's bodily movement, or perhaps earlier? According to my theory, the activity of the bullet flying through the air is part of a piece of available activity, and is therefore part of the action. It is part of a structure of smaller pieces of available activity and other pieces of activity that will occur if earlier pieces occur, which as a whole results in the president being shot.

In Chapter 1, when considering this sort of question, I distinguished between the action of making an attempt at shooting the president and the action of making sure of shooting the president. The latter includes checking to see if the first shot has worked and keeping on trying until the president is shot; whereas the former action is over before he is shot. But I now want to add that even when Oswald only has one shot to make he is not *just* making a shot at shooting the president (although he is also doing this); he is also shooting the president, and this includes the activity of the bullet flying through the air and striking the president.

Davidson's famous argument against this position (1980: 57–8), paraphrased to suit this case, runs as follows.

> After Oswald has squeezed his finger in such a way as to cause the shooting of the president, he has done his work; it only remains for the bullet to do its.

It is supposed to follow from this that the action cannot extend beyond the finger movement. But this is a mistaken step. According to my theory of action, after Oswald has squeezed his finger on the trigger, there is no further action for him to do. The rest is up to nature. However, this does not rule out the whole structure consisting in his squeezing the trigger, the gun firing, the bullet flying, etc., from being an action. After Oswald has squeezed his finger on the trigger, one action is over and no more actions are to come; but there is also an action which is still happening.

Hornsby (1980) also has an interesting argument against identifying actions with anything that goes outside the body. Hornsby first introduces the important distinction between transitive and intransitive bodily movements. An intransitive bodily movement (bodily movement$_I$) is what occurs when the body moves in a certain way. A transitive bodily movement (bodily movement$_T$) is what occurs when a subject moves their body in a certain way. Hornsby then wants to say that, although some actions are bodily movements$_T$, 'no actions are bodily movements$_I$' (1980: 5).

One argument she uses is that in answering the question, 'What did he do?', we can say 'He moved his finger,' but not 'His finger moved.' But, I think, that to conclude from this that no actions are bodily movements$_I$ is a mistake. Consider an analogous argument. Suppose a computer runs a program. In answering the question 'What did the computer do?', we can say 'It ran the program,' but not 'The program ran.' According to the structure of Hornsby's argument, we should be able to conclude that the transitive running of the program by the computer is distinct from the intransitive running of the program in the computer. But this conclusion does not look at all desirable. In both arguments, the question specifies a subject—him in the first argument and the computer in the second. An appropriate answer must use the same subject. But it does not follow that an inappropriate answer using a different subject must pick out a different event.

According to my account of processes, an intransitive process involves more than just the bare changes from one state to another. A bodily movement$_I$ may be a richly structured process with an underlying nature that essentially involves an agent. On the other hand, there is an event we might identify which is nothing more than the bare change or series of changes manifested by such a process in the body. It may be that this event is what Hornsby has in mind as a bodily movement$_I$. In that case, her conclusion that no actions are bodily movements$_I$ is quite right.

Hornsby goes on to argue that 'all actions that are movements$_T$ occur inside the body' (1980: 13). The argument goes as follows:

Where 'a' designates something in the category of *continuant* (rather than event), it is a necessary condition of the truth of 'a ϕ_T-s b' that a cause b to ϕ_I. In that case movements$_T$ of the body are *events that cause bodily movements*$_I$. (1980: 13)

I take it that there is a missing step in this argument which is that what makes it the case that a causes b to ϕ_I when a ϕ_T-s b is that a ϕ_T-ing b causes b to ϕ_I. This is not generally true given a rich conception of intransitive processes. We could accept that it is a necessary condition of the truth of 'the computer runs$_T$ the program' that the computer causes the program to run$_I$, while denying that the running$_T$ of the program is an event that causes the program to run$_I$. However, given the thinner conception of a movement$_I$ as an event of a bare change or series of changes, Hornsby's conclusion seems to be correct. The running$_T$ of the program does cause (or, better, result in) the changes associated with that process.

But to conclude, as Hornsby does, that the movement$_T$ must have its entire existence before the thinly conceived movement$_I$ is quite unjustified. It might be justified if the causation involved in movements$_T$ causing movements$_I$ was event-causation. In the standard model of event-causation, the event which is the cause must be over before the event which is the effect starts. Whether or not this model is correct, it does not apply here. The cause in this case is a process—it is the process of the agent moving their body, and the results of a process are stages that occur *during* the course of the process. The event which is the completion of a process will extend across the time in which the results of the process occur. The running$_T$ of a computer program results in variables changing values and so on, but the running$_T$ of the computer program is not over before these changes happen.

It should be possible to extend my account of action to an account of agency. An agent is something that produces actions. An action is the result of a teleological process. The thing that produces the results of a teleological process is a teleological mechanism. So it is a natural extension of my account of action to think of an agent in terms of a teleological mechanism.

I am not going to work out the details of such an account here. There would be a stronger and a weaker version of it. According to the weaker account, something counts as an agent in virtue of its activity being run by a teleological mechanism. The stronger account has it that the teleological mechanism itself *is* the agent. This stronger version might be a bit ambitious—it would depend on an account of the identity conditions of mechanisms—but it is a gratifyingly simple account of agency. According to the stronger account, we are all essentially teleological mechanisms—machines which operate by resulting in what should happen according to some method of practical justification.

A worry one might have with this account of what an agent is, is that the externalism about action that I have been arguing for might transfer to an externalism about what an agent is. I have argued that actions do not take place entirely within the agent, but this had better not mean that the mechanism underlying the production of actions does not exist entirely within the agent. Otherwise, what is essential to an agent will include something quite outside that agent. This is a highly undesirable, and possibly, contradictory, conclusion. Whatever one thinks about the social construction of agency, one does not want Oswald's gun to be an essential part of Oswald, the agent.

The presence of Oswald's gun is part of the underlying conditions of the process of Oswald shooting the president. But that does not mean that it is part of the underlying conditions of the teleological process that results in that process of Oswald shooting the president. The same teleological process would be happening even without the gun. Without the presence of the gun that teleological process would have quite different results—quite different actions would ensue. But it would be the same teleological process, and be run by the same underlying mechanism. So the worry that my externalism about action must be reflected in an incoherent externalism about agency is unfounded.

B. INTENTIONS AND BELIEFS

Most accounts of action are accounts in terms of intentions (or desires) and beliefs. Mine is not. This means that I can use my account of action to construct an account of intentions and beliefs. I call this account Teleological Behaviourism. I think that Teleological Behaviourism is an extremely powerful and new way of

approaching the philosophy of mind quite generally.[2] Here I am
only going to make a few sketchy moves towards an account of
beliefs and intentions to substantiate my claim that I can turn the
standard theories of action upside down. I think that some suggestion of the power of this approach will emerge.

I define beliefs and intentions as follows.

> An agent believes that P if and only if a teleological process
> producing the agent's behaviour is governed by a method of
> practical justification which in the circumstances works on the
> assumption that P is true.

> An agent intends to achieve G if and only if a teleological
> process producing the agent's behaviour is governed by a
> method of practical justification which in the circumstances
> works on the assumption that G is to be achieved.

Given what I said about working assumptions at the end of the
previous chapter, there are two ways that a method might work on
some assumption. That assumption might be a fact which is established by the process governed by that method and which the
method employs as an input. Or, the assumption may be embedded
as a fixed point in the method. If my account of belief is right, then
this means that there are two possible sorts of situation underlying
someone believing a proposition. Either the subject has established
that proposition to be a fact, or that proposition is embedded as a
working assumption—an unstable distortion—in the method that
governs the way a subject works.[3]

A belief can be formed irrationally—this is to be understood in
terms of an embedded working assumption becoming part of the
method of practical justification governing the agent. Or it can be
established rationally, albeit possibly from irrationally formed beliefs. This is to be understood as the result of the teleological
process progressing. What distinguishes establishing beliefs from
establishing facts is that the process which progresses in the former
case is one governed by a method of practical justification which
embeds (possibly false) working assumptions. As I remarked in

    [2] Larry Wright (1976) and Bennett (1976) have accounts which are in some ways
similar, but their accounts of teleological explanation do not give them the resources
which mine does.
    [3] Note the relationship between this claim and the disjunctive approach to ap-
pearances discussed in Chapter 1, Section C.

Chapter 4, Section G, such a method can only count as a method of practical justification if the *goals* (as opposed to the means) are conditioned by the working assumptions. So the method recommends, as goals, doing what would be justified on the assumption that the working assumptions are true. And progress with respect to a process governed by such a method consists in establishing what would be the case on the assumption that the working assumptions are true. When the process has progressed with respect to the fact that P would be the case given the working assumptions (i.e. this fact—that P would be the case given the working assumptions—has been established), then the agent is working on the assumption that P is the case (i.e. the belief that P has been established). This working assumption does not have to be *embedded* in the method of practical justification governing the agent; rather, it can be seen as the result of making progress with a teleological process which is governed by a method of practical justification which embeds other working assumptions.

Let me try to illustrate this account of beliefs and intentions. Consider my false belief that in a correctly wired-up plug the blue wire should be connected to the live terminal. According to this account, I have such a belief if and only if my activity is governed by a method of practical justification which works on the assumption that this proposition is true. Similarly, I have the intention to have the plug wired up properly over the next few minutes if and only if my activity is governed by a method of practical justification which works on the assumption that the plug is to be wired up properly in the next few minutes. If I have both this intention and this belief, and I have reached that point where the wires are to be connected up, then I will attach the blue wire to the live terminal.

However, just having this belief and this intention does not guarantee that I will attach the blue wire to the live terminal. Suppose that the method governing my activity has embedded in it a false working assumption, namely the proposition that a screwdriver can be found, when in fact a screwdriver cannot be found. Part of the means that is recommended by the method may be to find a screwdriver. The rest of the means may be to take the plug apart, attach the wires properly, etc. All goes well until it becomes established that a screwdriver cannot be found. In such a situation the method which has the working assumption that a screwdriver can be found can give no recommendation; the working assump-

tion lapses and the method adapts. If it is established that there is
no way of wiring up the plug correctly in the next few minutes then
situational appreciation will adapt the goal, perhaps to the goal of
wiring up the plug later and buying a screwdriver now. From this
point, the method of practical justification governing my behaviour
does not work on the assumption that the plug is to be wired up
properly in the next few minutes and we can say that I no longer
have that intention. I still have the false belief about the correct way
to attach the blue wire, however. Although that working assumption is having no effect at the moment, it would be manifested if
someone asked me how to wire up a plug correctly, or gave me a
screwdriver, etc.

This account explains the relationship between intentions and
plans observed by many philosophers (see especially Brand 1984
and Bratman 1987). Having an intention to achieve G means
having one's activity governed by a method of practical justification
which works on the assumption that G is to be achieved. A reasonably sophisticated method of practical justification will involve
situational appreciation. This means that its recommendation of a
goal will be subject to its also being able to recommend that there
is an available course of action—a plan. This suggests that if a goal
is recommended by a method of practical justification, so is a plan
to achieve that goal.

There are exceptions, however. If the goal of the intention is
some basic activity, then there is no need for a plan; or the plan will
be 'Just do it!'. More interesting cases emerge if it is established that
there is a way of achieving the goal, but it is not established what
that way is. Perhaps there are two available means and it is not yet
established which is better. Or, perhaps there is a quite irrational
belief—an embedded working assumption—that a means exists. In
such a case one can confidently intend to achieve a goal without
having any plan in mind.

Associated with the behaviourism of my account, there is the
principle that it makes no sense to attribute any beliefs and intentions to oneself or others if these states are not manifestable somehow. It might be thought that a problem is posed for my account if
someone who has no belief concerning the truth of B decides
nevertheless to act just as if B were true anyway. But, according to
this hypothesis, the person would have to act as if B were true even
in situations where a lot depended on getting it right. Now, to make

sense of this situation at all, there must be some reason for the agent to be behaving in this way. For, if not, then there could be no motivation for denying that the agent believed that *B*. But if there is such a reason, then we can devise a situation in which that reason fails to hold and the true nature of the agent's behaviour is manifested.

A related question is that of *dormant* beliefs and intentions. Can my account distinguish them from merely *potential* beliefs and intentions? By a dormant belief I mean a belief that is not currently motivating any behaviour at all. For example, a few minutes ago it was true that I believed that grass was green, but having that belief was not manifested in my behaviour. I can be said to have had that belief because it had the potential to be manifested in my behaviour had the situation been appropriate to that.

The process resulting in my behaviour can be said to be governed by a method of practical justification which works with that assumption rather than by one which does not, because, given no change in the underlying nature of that process, if I were in a situation where the results of the method of practical justification were sensitive to this, and no information concerning the colour of grass was rationally available, the results of the process would conform to the assumption that grass was green. The same would be true if I was asleep at the time. If what I said about the dormant stages of the freeze–thaw process in Chapter 2, Section B, was right, then my teleological processes are still happening when I am asleep.

On the other hand, that there is a solitary dandelion in the middle of the lawn also had the potential to be manifested in my behaviour. But I did not believe it. The difference is that before the fact that there is a solitary dandelion in the middle of the lawn can be manifested in my behaviour I have to look out at the lawn, whereas no such information-gathering behaviour is required for the fact that the grass is green to be manifested. Some facts will need to be established of course even in this case—but not the fact that grass is green.

Now consider potential beliefs which require a certain amount of reasoning in order to be formed and then manifested in behaviour. For example, in a game of chess I did not believe when I started thinking about the move that I should sacrifice my queen, but after a few minutes of thinking I did believe this. Suppose a situation had arisen when I first started thinking about the move in which I had no more time to think before acting. In other words any more establishing of the facts about the best move was ruled out. The result would not have been in accordance with a method of practical justification working on the assumption that the queen should be sacrificed. (Note that even if I hit on the move by luck I would not put money on it.) There is no failure in operating conditions that can account for this failure. So my behaviour at that point is not governed by such a method.

So it looks as if my theory accounts for the distinction between actually having beliefs that are not currently being manifested and only potentially having beliefs. Can it work as well for the same distinction with intentions? Cases where an agent only potentially has an intention (e.g. were they to perceive some relevant facts or do some relevant reasoning) are ruled out as real cases of intention on my account in just the same way as potential beliefs are. However, it might be thought that the notion of a dormant intention is more problematic than the notion of a dormant belief.

Suppose that I form the intention to have a massive birthday party on my eightieth birthday. On my account, this must involve having a current mechanism capable of producing results *now* that would be practically justified on the assumption that I am to have such a party. But there is an apparent objection, which is that having this intention may have no way of being manifested in current behaviour. According to the thinking behind this objection, one has the intention in virtue of having certain thoughts—mental reminders to be picked up in the future—and these need only be tied to behaviour in the distant future in order to constitute the having of a real intention.

However, suppose the situation arises in which it becomes established that my memory will not be sufficient to the task. If I really have this intention to have an eightieth birthday party, I will act on it now by making an actual note of the intention and somehow making it difficult for myself to get out of the commitment when the time comes. If I would not act in that way now, then it really makes no sense to say that I have such an intention now. So dormant intentions, like dormant beliefs, should be thought of in terms of current mechanisms and processes. Even when the characteristic stages are likely to be manifested only some time in the future, situations can arise which force them to be manifested right away.

C. IRRATIONALITY

The following argument might be thought to be fatal to my account of beliefs and intentions. Beliefs and intentions are individuated at the level of sense and not at the level of truth conditions. For example, suppose that Sarah believes that John is hungry. John is Julie, though Sarah is not aware of this. So John is hungry if and only if Julie is hungry. The two propositions are true in all the same circumstances, yet beliefs having these propositions as their contents are not identical, for we can consistently suppose that Sarah does not believe that Julie is hungry. On my account, roughly, Sarah believes that John is hungry if and only if Sarah does what would be justified were it the case that John is hungry. But this means that Sarah does what would be justified were it the case that Julie is hungry, and so believes that Julie is hungry. This contradicts the hypothesis; so there must be something wrong with my account.

However, in trying to make this argument work, I have crucially misrepresented my own account. It is an important feature of the account that beliefs and intentions are indeed individuated at the level of sense and not at the level of truth conditions. The condition for Sarah believing a proposition is *not* that Sarah must do what would be justified were the proposition true. Rather, it is that the theoretical method of practical justification which governs what Sarah does works on the *assumption* that the proposition is true. The assumption that John is hungry is not the same assumption as the assumption that Julie is hungry even if they are true or false together in all possible worlds. If one assumption is determining the results of a theoretical method, there is no guarantee that the same results will be described by that method as would be described if the other one was determining the method. The method, in this case, does not have the resources to start working on the assumption that Julie is hungry even if it is working on the assumption that John is hungry.

A more acute sort of case occurs with the possibility of believing logically inconsistent propositions. Here is another argument against my account. Although it is logically inconsistent that $8^2 = 36$, I may believe it due to some confusion. (If this seems too unlikely, think of a harder sum.) From the assumption that $8^2 = 36$ everything follows. So, acting on the assumption that $8^2 = 36$

involves acting on the assumption that everything is true, which is impossible. Again the hypothesis seems to be contradicted.

In some senses, it is true that from an inconsistent proposition everything follows. One sense in which this is true is that everything is *semantically entailed* by an inconsistent proposition. For every sentence, S, there is no possible situation in which $8^2 = 36$ is true and S is false. Also, and perhaps more worryingly, in any proof system which captures the axioms of arithmetic, every single formula is entailed by the formula expressing $8^2 = 36$.

However, a process governed by a method of practical justification working with that assumption need not establish all such entailments straightaway. It establishes them as it needs them. So, if someone asks me what 8^2 is equal to, and I am governed by a method which works on the assumption that $8^2 = 36$, assuming that the method also recommends that I give the right answer, I will say '36'. Similarly, if I am working on a mathematical problem, it may make sense according to that method to substitute 8^2 for 36, etc.

It is easy to think of circumstances in which the method will collapse. If the fact that $6^2 = 36$ is established, it may make sense to substitute 8^2 for 36 establishing the belief that $6^2 = 8^2$, and then the belief that $6 = 8$ might be established. In such circumstances the method of practical justification governing my behaviour yields a direct contradiction (that I say that 6 is equal to 8 and I do not say that 6 is equal to 8) and must adapt. For a method to be a method of *description*, as a method of practical justification is supposed to be, it must not yield a direct contradiction. So the belief that $8^2 = 36$ is unstable. If a situation arises where working with that assumption yields a direct contradiction, then that working assumption must be withdrawn from the method. But, if no such situation arises, the method can have it as a working assumption.

The key point is that a process governed by a method of practical justification is unlike a proof system in that it allows a distinction between what gets established by the process and what theoretically might get established by the process.[4] It establishes results in a particular order that the method itself may determine as justified.

---

[4] Harman (1986) stresses the distinction between systems of reasoning and proof systems. His approach is internalist, but stripped of its internalism his notion of reasoning is close to my notion of a method of practical justification.

It may also establish results in an unpredictable order through exploratory activity. Even when a contradiction is theoretically establishable by the process, it does not follow that it will be established. Proof systems do not have this dynamic nature (though they might do if they employed non-monotonic logic).

This is why it is possible to hold an inconsistent triad of beliefs. For example, suppose I believe that I will be abroad for the second half of August on holiday. Suppose also that absent-mindedly I arrange to meet someone at home on 20 August, and I believe that I will keep the appointment. And suppose finally that I know that these two things are incompatible. On my account, the fact that I believe these three propositions just is the fact that I am run by a teleological mechanism that is governed by a method of practical justification which works on the assumptions that I will be abroad in the second half of August, I will be at home on 20 August, and these two things are mutually incompatible.

No problems emerge where the rational course of action depends on just one or two of these inconsistent propositions. Suppose the question arises of whether I should cancel the newspaper delivery for the second half of August. If I am working on the assumption that I will be abroad in the second half of August, then I should cancel the papers. That I am also working on the assumption that I am meeting someone at home on 20 August is not *directly* relevant since the question has not yet been asked of me that would involve this working assumption. Similarly, suppose the question arises whether I should do some preparation for the meeting. How this preparation should be done is determined by the assumption that I am meeting this person at home on 20 August. It is quite possible that I both cancel the papers and do this preparation for the meeting at home.

But what about situations where the inconsistency bites? For example, suppose that I need to tell someone whether I will be abroad on holiday at the time when I am due to have the meeting. The question makes both working assumptions directly relevant. According to one, I should say that I will be abroad; while, according to the other, I should say that I will not be. This means that if such a question is put to me, my method must adapt. The method working with inconsistent assumptions is therefore unstable, but it is not impossible. Note that it is part of general intellectual exploration to ask oneself such questions, although it may not be possible to set up a method that guarantees that the right questions will be asked so that inconsistency is exposed.

This approach to inconsistency does not countenance the possibility of believing a pair of directly contradictory propositions, P and not-P. For there is no situation where a teleological process could have results that were justified by some method on the assumption that P and not-P are both true. In any situation where it was relevant whether P, it would also be relevant whether not-P. In any such situation, the method would collapse into direct contradiction. In the case of the inconsistent triad of working assumptions, there are some situations where some but not all of the working assumptions are employed by the method. This is not the case for the directly contradictory pair of working assumptions.

This is desirable, since it does seem to be absurd to attribute anyone with beliefs in both a proposition and its negation. However, problems for my account seem to arise if it is possible for me to be in a state in which in certain situations I do what would be justified given the assumption that P, and in other situations I do what would be justified given the assumption that not-P. According to my account, we should say that I do not believe either P or not-P. However, it may be more natural to claim that in some sense I believe them both. It might be thought that deep down I believe that P, but in terms of my more superficial behaviour patterns I believe that not-P.

One way that this might be explained is if I really believe that P, but also believe that I should believe that not-P. The belief that I should believe that not-P manifests itself in very similar ways to the ways that the simple belief that not-P manifests itself. For example, in situations involving communication, it may be rational to assert not-P rather than P. My purpose in communicating may be to impress or to conform rather than to tell the truth.

If my belief that I should believe not-P is the belief that, according to the generally accepted theoretical method, it is rational to believe that not-P, then there is no actual irrationality here. A more interesting case is where I believe that, according to *my own theoretical method*, I should believe that not-P, nevertheless I believe that P. One way that this might happen is if my belief about the workings of my own theoretical method is false. For example, I may believe that I share the beliefs of my twin, and for this reason come to believe that according to my theoretical method I should believe that not-*P* (since my twin does), nevertheless I believe that *P*. This case is equivalent to having a false belief about my beliefs. It is an unstable position to be in, but it is a situation quite consistent with my account.

But consider a more difficult case. Suppose that I am presented with the information that I have an Oedipal complex, but I do not believe it, because then I would have to accept that I am not the sort of person I want to be. This reveals a kind of irrationality that looks like a real problem for my account. Assume the operational conditions of my teleological mechanism are satisfied, and that I am clearly presented with the information that I do have an Oedipal complex. Then, in those situations where this fact is relevant to what my method of practical justification recommends, it is rationally available to my method of practical justification, which must then work on the assumption that it is true. Yet, this means that I believe I have an Oedipal complex. This contradicts the initial hypothesis.

This sort of case (following Pears 1984) can be described as motivated irrationality. I think that the right way to interpret it is to deny the step between the following positions:

A. In those situations where the truth or falsity of *P* would affect the results of a method of practical justification, the method of practical justification would work on the assumption that *P* is true.

B. The method of practical justification works on the assumption that *P* is true.

In this sort of case of motivated irrationality the agent makes sure that in no situations does the rationality of their behaviour depend on the truth of *P*. In the example under consideration, I am not in fact motivated by the goal of speaking the truth about myself; so it is quite justified for me to deny that I have an Oedipal complex. It remains true that if the justification of some behaviour depended on the fact that I have an Oedipal complex, that behaviour would have to result, given that my behaviour is governed by the appropriate method of practical justification. But I make sure that my structure of goals is such that no such behaviour could be required. I structure my goals in such a way that avoidance of the issue is ensured— this is what psychotherapists would call 'denial'. So it is not the case that my behaviour is governed by a method of practical justification that recommends what would be justified on the assumption that I have an Oedipal complex. There is no situation where that aspect of the supposed method could manifest itself. So I do not believe I have an Oedipal complex.

The restructuring of goals necessary to avoid having this belief may well leave me with inconsistencies in my beliefs. But they will be of the unproblematic kind rather than a straight face off between *P* and not-*P*. It may also make it difficult for me to build up structures of goals. It is a commonly observed psychological fact that people with motivated irrationality may often fail to make very much of themselves. In the extreme case I will be rendered incapable of doing almost anything at all, because avoiding having the belief about myself will be impossible unless I do nothing. (Note that good psychological therapy is more concerned with undermining the motivation for not believing that *P* than with battering away at the client with the fact that *P*.)

Given my definitions of belief and intention, intending to achieve *G* is the same as believing that *G* is to be achieved. This seems to rule out automatically a sort of acrasia that many philosophers think is a natural phenomenon—namely believing that *G* should not be achieved but intending to achieve it anyway (see e.g. Mele 1987).

This phenomenon can be explained on my account by distinguishing the belief that *G* should be achieved from the belief that *G* is to be achieved. I take it that this is something like Davidson's strategy in 'How is Weakness of the Will Possible?' (1980: essay 2). As with the case of apparently contradictory beliefs considered earlier, the belief that *G* should be achieved might be a belief about some other method of justification, in which case there is no irrationality here at all. Or, it might be about the subject's own method of justification, in which case it is just a false belief, but involves no direct contradiction; I may believe that *G* is to be achieved and believe that I believe that *G* is not to be achieved because I am deceived about my own motivations.

One way this might happen is when a subject's behaviour is governed by a method of practical justification which embeds the working assumption that *G* is to be achieved, though it *follows* from the method that *G* is not to be achieved. This would need to be explained in the same way as the example of the Oedipal complex. Although it would follow from my method of practical justification in certain situations and given certain other goals that G is to be achieved, I can still be governed by a method that embeds the working assumption that G is not to be achieved as long as I avoid those situations and goals. In particular, I may have to avoid thinking about it too much.

This analysis seems to work quite well for some cases of incontinently smoking a cigarette. Suppose that the method of practical justification that governs my behaviour would recommend that I do not smoke that cigarette if certain other claims were established—e.g. I am resolved and am to remain resolved not to be a smoker; smoking a cigarette will destroy my resolve not to be a smoker; so smoking this will destroy my resolve not to be a smoker; so I am not to smoke this. If I can avoid establishing these claims— e.g. by refusing to listen to someone who is lecturing me on the subject—I can be governed by a method which works on the assumption that I must remain *resolved* not to be a smoker and also on the assumption that I am to smoke this.

D. BEHAVIOURISM

Behaviourism is not a very popular philosophical doctrine these days. Galen Strawson's recent book, *Mental Reality*, begins boldly with the following claim: 'Behaviorism is dead. No one still believes that mental concepts can be satisfactorily analysed just in terms of behavior and dispositions to behavior' (1994: p. xi). But this claim, at least, I can quite easily refute. According to my account, which I proudly call 'Teleological Behaviourism', what it is to believe P (or intend to achieve G) is to be driven by a mechanism whose working is governed by a method of practical justification which works on the assumption that P (or that G is to be achieved). This is an instance of the 'truly extraordinary view that the whole story about what it is for a being to be in a certain mental state, or to be the locus of a certain mental occurrence, is just that it is behaving in certain ways or is disposed to behave in certain ways' (G. Strawson 1994: 30).

Ryle, of course, held this view too (1949: 199):

To talk of a person's mind is . . . to talk of the person's abilities, liabilities and inclinations to do and undergo certain sorts of things, and of the doing and undergoing of these things in the ordinary world.

Armstrong also held this behaviourist view (1968: 82). 'The concept of a mental state is primarily the concept of *a state of the person apt for bringing about a certain sort of behaviour.*' Armstrong vehemently denied being a behaviourist, since he took behaviourism (with some historical justification) to involve the denial that mental processes are inner processes. But I want to separate questions about the correct analysis of dispositions from the question of the truth of behaviourism, which I take to be the claim that mental states are to be accounted for in terms of behavioural dispositions. Armstrong thought that having a behavioural disposition is to be identified with being in a certain physical state. Ryle not only denied this identification but also denied that having a behavioural disposition was a current *fact* about a person. In my account of processes and capacities in Chapter 2, I argued that having a disposition requires the satisfaction of some set of underlying conditions, but I feel no pressure to *identify* having the disposition with having those conditions satisfied. Despite these differences, I want to characterize all three views as behaviourist.

A question for a behaviourist is how and to what extent the behavioural dispositions that constitute some sort of mental state should be spelled out in an account of that mental state. There is a clear dilemma here. If the behaviourist thinks that the disposition should be completely specified, then the account collapses if no finite specification can be arrived at. But, as Ryle himself observed, 'the higher-grade dispositions of people with which this inquiry is largely concerned are, in general, not single-track dispositions, but dispositions the exercises of which are indefinitely heterogeneous' (1949: 44). It is by now a familiar point that the belief that it is raining cannot be captured by the disposition to take an umbrella when one goes out. Nor can it be captured by a more detailed specification of the disposition, since it will always be possible to think of some situation not included in the specification where the belief may be manifested.

If, on the other hand, the behaviourist does not require a complete specification of the behavioural disposition in an account of a certain kind of mental state, then the account itself is not complete.

This may be alright for open-ended concepts, like that of pride. But the concept of belief seems to be more determinate than that. We want an account of belief that says what sort of behavioural disposition constitutes believing something.

Behaviourists who are functionalists may feel that they avoid the first horn of the dilemma by insisting that the specification of the behavioural disposition corresponding to some belief is not only going to be extremely complex, it is also going to be holistic. So the specification of the behavioural disposition corresponding to some belief will include mention of other beliefs, desires, intentions, etc. This means that what is being analysed behaviouristically is not a single mental state, but a set of mental states. The heterogeneity of behavioural dispositions corresponding to a single mental state that Ryle observed may be explained by the functionalist in terms of the multiplicity of other mental states that could be interacting with the one in question. When all the mental states are put together, it may not seem so wrong to think of the whole set as corresponding to a single-track behavioural disposition.

I think that McDowell has put paid to this thought (1985). He argues that any specification of a behavioural disposition corresponding to a mental state or set of mental states must respect what Davidson has called 'the constitutive ideal of rationality' (Davidson 1980: 223). Then he claims that 'it would be a fantasy to suppose that the full normative force of the concept [of rationality]... could be captured in a structure specifiable from outside intentional content' (McDowell 1985: 391). This means that there can be no complete functionalist specification of behavioural dispositions corresponding to a mental state or set of mental states.

If one is a behaviourist impressed by this argument, then a natural move is to suppose that the correct specification of a behavioural disposition should *invoke* the concept of rationality. The sort of account that would emerge is the following:

> A subject has a certain set of mental states if and only if there is a way of construing rationality so that the subject is disposed to do what would be rational given all those mental states.

This is very like what Ryle says. 'Knowing *how*, then, is a disposition, but not a single-track disposition like a reflex or a habit. Its exercises are observances of rules or canons or the applications of

criteria' (1949: 46). Although still behaviourist, this account has
lost all the reductive aspirations of standard functionalist accounts.
The trouble with this account as it stands is that it has nothing to
say about what it is to be in one mental state rather than another.
The account says nothing explicitly about what it is to believe
something, for instance.

I think that we can remedy this if we allow an externalist conception of rationality. The sort of account we could get is the
following:

> A subject has a certain set of beliefs and intentions if and only
> if there is a way of construing rationality (externalistically) so
> that the subject is disposed to do what would be rational given
> all the beliefs are true and the intentions right.

Allowing an externalist conception of rationality gives us a way of
avoiding having holism as an explicit part of the account. We need
only allow that a conception of rationality might work on false
assumptions while still being a conception of rationality; then we
get the following account of belief.

> A subject believes that *P* if and only if there is a way of
> construing rationality (externalistically and as embodying
> working assumptions) so that the subject is disposed to do
> what would be rational on the assumption that *P*.

This is a reductive account of belief in the sense that there are no
mental states *mentioned* on the right-hand side of the biconditional.
However, concepts that are employed on the right-hand side of the
biconditional include that of a subject, that of doing, and that of a
conception of rationality. Arguably, these concepts depend on mental state concepts, in which case, the account is not reductive in any
strong sense.

The use of the concept of a subject on the right-hand side is not
an important problem for reductivism. It appears on the left-hand
side too and can be factored out. We could say that a *thing* believes
P if and only if that thing has the appropriate behavioural disposition. Much more serious is the presence of the concept of *doing*.
Hornsby (1986) argues that, because behaviourist accounts must
refer to behaviour, any reductivist ambitions they might have are
squashed. She argues that there is an equivocation between two

conceptions of behaviour in the thinking of reductive behaviourists (or functionalists). According to one conception, behaviour is intentional action; according to the other, it is merely bodily activity. Hornsby argues that the sort of behaviour that should figure in the specification of a behavioural disposition corresponding to a mental state or set of mental states is intentional action. But the concept of intentional action is a mental one, and so the reduction of the mental to the non-mental is thwarted. Only if the sort of behaviour that figures in the specification of a behavioural disposition is mere bodily activity can behaviourism be reductive.

Hornsby's argument against the conception of behaviour which figures in a behaviourist account of mental states being that of mere bodily activity only works against a functionalist sort of behaviourism. She argues that some activity, φ-ing, can figure in a functionalist account of mental states 'only if agents have some beliefs in the ascription of which φ-ing could be mentioned. So functionalists are not in fact entitled to use whatever bodily movement terms they like; their resources can include only such terms as could be used in giving the contents of agents' mental states' (1986: 104). This must be right. The scheme of rationality that is implicit in a functionalist specification is an *internalist* one relating inputs, outputs, beliefs, and intentions (or desires). For inputs, outputs, beliefs, and intentions to be internalistically rationally co-ordinated, the inputs must be such that the beliefs and intentions are about them. But this restriction rules out there being any high level of detail in the appropriate specification of the behaviour, since there is so little detail in the specification of the content of any of the beliefs about our bodily activity. 'It seems that a person can act as a result of having beliefs and desires, while having next to nothing in the way of beliefs about how her body moves when she acts' (Hornsby 1986: 104).

This argument is sound against a reductive functionalist account employing implicitly an internalist conception of rationality. For reasons mentioned earlier, I think that this account must be false anyway. But the argument has no force against the reductive behaviourist account which explicitly employs an externalist conception of rationality. A subject can discriminate between different bits of bodily activity in their action at a much finer level of detail than they can in their descriptions. At this level of detail, inputs and outputs can be externalistically rationally co-ordinated, even though they cannot be internalistically rationally co-ordinated with beliefs and desires.

The reductive behaviourist account that we have ended up with is the following:

> A thing believes that P if and only if there is a way of construing rationality (externalistically and as embodying working assumptions) so that it is disposed to produce that activity which would be rational on the assumption that P.

This is almost identical to the account which I have worked up towards through this book and which I call Teleological Behaviourism:

> A mechanism is associated with the belief that P if and only if its working is governed by a method of practical justification which works on the assumption that P.

This would be a thoroughly reductive account were it not for the mention of a method of practical justification (or a way of construing rationality). Given my externalist notion of practical justification, it is not clear that someone needs to employ the ability to attribute mental states to the subject in question or indeed to anyone at all in order to employ the conceptions of a method of practical justification. So, if my account in Chapter 4 of practical justification is on the right lines, then a reductive account of mental states is possible. But this is not a reductive account of intentionality—i.e. of what it is to represent things in thought or in language. That is because I have not sought a way to reduce the notion of a normative method of description, which is a (possibly *the*) basic intentional concept. I do not attempt to do what McDowell in the earlier quotation claimed to be a fantasy, namely to capture the full normative force of the concept of rationality from outside intentional content. So I have not tried to capture the concept of mental intentionality from outside either. But what I have done is to give an account of *mental* intentional states in terms of intentional concepts that apply to *language*; and this is a reduction of sorts.

REFERENCES

Achinstein, P. (1977), 'Function Statements', *Philosophy of Science*, 44: 341–67.

——(1981), 'Can there be a Model of Explanation?', *Theory and Decision*, 13: 201–27, repr. in Ruben (1993: 136–59).

——(1983), *The Nature of Explanation* (New York).

Annas, J. (1982), 'Aristotle's Inefficient Causes', *Philosophical Quarterly*, 32: 311–26.

Anscombe, E. (1957), *Intentions* (Oxford).

——(1971), *Causality and Determination* (Cambridge).

Aristotle (1984 edn.), *The Complete Works of Aristotle* ed. J. Barnes (Princeton).

Armstrong, D. (1968), *A Materialist Theory of the Mind* (London).

Ayers, M. (1968), *The Refutation of Determinism* (London).

Bennett, J. (1976), *Linguistic Behaviour* (Cambridge).

Bergson, H. (1960 edn.), *Creative Evolution*, tr. A. Mitchell (London).

Bigelow, J., and Pargetter, R. (1987), 'Functions', *Journal of Philosophy*, 84: 181–96.

Boorse, C. (1976), 'Wright on Functions', *Philosophical Review*, 85: 70–86.

Brand, M. (1984), *Intending and Acting* (Cambridge, Mass.).

Brandom, R. (1994), *Making it Explicit* (Cambridge, Mass.).

Bratman, M. (1987), *Intentions, Plans and Practical Reason* (Cambridge, Mass.).

Brody, B. (1972), 'Towards an Aristotelian Theory of Scientific Explanation', *Philosophy of Science*, 39: 20–31, repr. in Ruben (1993: 113–27).

Cartwright, N. (1983), *How the Laws of Physics Lie* (Oxford).

Charles, D. (1984), *Aristotle's Philosophy of Action* (London).

Charlton, W. (1991), 'Teleology and Mental States', *Proceedings of the Aristotelian Society*, suppl. vol. 65: 17–32.

Child, W. (1994), *Causality, Interpretation and the Mind* (Oxford).

Chisholm, R. M. (1966), 'Freedom and Action', in K. Lehrer (ed.), *Freedom and Interpretation* (New York), 11–44.

Clark, A. (1989), *Microcognition* (Cambridge, Mass.).

Comrie, B. (1976), *Aspect* (Cambridge).

Cooper, J. (1987), 'Hypothetical Necessity and Natural Teleology', in A. Gotthelf and G. Lennox (eds.), *Philosophical Issues in Aristotle's Biology* (Cambridge), 243–74.

Cummins, R. (1975), 'Functional Analysis', *Journal of Philosophy*, 72: 741–65.

Danto, A. (1973), *Analytical Philosophy of Action* (Cambridge).

Davidson, D. (1980), *Essays on Actions and Events* (Oxford).

Dennett, D. (1984), *Elbow Room* (Cambridge, Mass.).

——(1987), *The Intentional Stance* (Cambridge, Mass.).

——(1991), *Consciousness Explained* (Boston).

Dretske, F. (1988), *Explaining Behaviour* (Cambridge, Mass.).

Evans, G. (1985), *Collected Papers* (Oxford).

Floistad (1982) (ed.), *Contemporary Philosophy*, iii. *Philosophy of Action* (The Hague).

Galton, A. (1984), *The Logic of Aspect* (Oxford).

Gill, K. (1993), 'On the Metaphysical Distinction between Processes and Events', *Canadian Journal of Philosophy*, 23: 365–84.

Goldman, A. (1970), *A Theory of Human Action* (Princeton).

——(1976), 'Discrimination and Perceptual Knowledge', *Journal of Philosophy*, 73: 771–91.

Gotthelf, A. (1987), 'Aristotle's Conception of Final Causation', in A. Gotthelf and G. Lennox (eds.), *Philosophical Issues in Aristotle's Biology* (Cambridge), 204–42.

Gould, S., and Lewontin, R. (1979), 'The Spardrels of San Marcos and the Panglossian Program', *Proceedings of the Royal Society of London*, 205: 281–8.

Graham, D. W. (1980), 'States, and Performances', *Philosophical Quarterly*, 30: 117–30.

Griffiths, P. (1993), 'Functional Analysis and Proper Functions', *British Journal of the Philosophy of Science*, 44: 409–22.

Harman, G. (1986), *Change in View* (Cambridge, Mass.).

Harré, R., and Madden, E. (1975), *Causal Powers* (Oxford).

Hegel, G. W. F. (1989 edn.), *Hegel Selections*, ed. M. Inwood (New York).

Hempel, C. (1965), 'Aspects of Scientific Explanation', in *Aspects of Scientific Explanation and Other Essays in the Philosophy of Science* (New York).

Hesse, M. (1963), *Models and Analogies in Science* (London).

Hinton, J. M. (1973), *Experiences* (Oxford).

Hofstadter, D. (1982), 'Can Creativity be Mechanized', *Scientific American*, 247 (Oct.), 20–9.

Hornsby, J. (1980), *Actions* (London).

——(1986), 'Physicalist Thinking and Conceptions of Behaviour', in P. Pettit and J. McDowell (eds.), *Subject, Thought and Context* (Oxford), 95–115.

Hume, D. (1888 edn.), *A Treatise of Human Nature* (Oxford).

Hursthouse, R. (1991), 'Arational Actions', *Journal of Philosophy*, 88: 57–68.

Kant, I. (1948 edn.), *The Moral Law*, ed. H. Paton (London).

Kenny, A. (1963), *Action, Emotion and Will* (London).

——(1975), *Will, Freedom and Power* (Oxford).

Kim, J. (1987), 'Explanatory Realism, Causal Realism and Explanatory Exclusion', *Midwest Studies in Philosophy*, 12: 225–39, repr. in Ruben (1993: 228–45).

Kitcher, P. (1989), 'Explanatory Unification and the Causal Structure of the World', in Kitcher and Salmon (1989: 410–505).

——and Salmon, W. (1989) (eds.), *Scientific Explanation* (Minneapolis).

Lepore, E., and McLaughlin, B. (1985) (eds.), *Actions and Events* (Oxford).

Lewis, D. (1986), 'Causal Explanation', in his *Philosophical Papers*, ii (Oxford), 214–20, repr. in Ruben (1993: 182–206).

Lipton, P. (1990), 'Contrastive Explanation', in D. Knowles (ed.) *Explanation and its Limits* (Cambridge), repr. in Ruben (1993: 207–27).

Lyotard, F. (1984 edn.), *The Post Modern Condition: A Report on Knowledge* (Manchester).

McCann, H. (1979), 'Nominals, Facts and Two Conceptions of Events', *Philosophical Studies*, 35: 129–49.

McCarthy, T. (1977), 'On an Aristotelian Model of Scientific Explanation', *Philosophy of Science*, 44: 159–66, repr. in Ruben (1993: 128–35).

McDowell, J. (1978), 'Are Moral Requirements Hypothetical Imperatives?', *Proceedings of the Aristotelian Society*, suppl. vol. 52: 13–29.

——(1982), 'Criteria, Defeasibility and Knowledge', *Proceedings of the British Academy*, 68: 455–79.

——(1985), 'Functionalism and Anomalous Monism', in Lepore and McLaughlin (1985: 387–98).

——(1987), 'In Defense of Modesty', in B. Taylor (ed.), *Michael Dummett: Contributions to Philosophy* (Dordrecht).

Melden, A. I. (1961), *Free Action* (London).

Mele, A. (1987), *Irrationality* (Oxford).

——(1992), *Springs of Action* (Oxford).

Millikan, R. G. (1984), *Language, Truth and Other Biological Categories* (Cambridge, Mass.).

——(1993), *White Queen Psychology and Other Essays for Alice* (Cambridge, Mass.).

Morton, A. (1975), 'Because He Thought He Had Insulted Him', *Journal of Philosophy*, 72: 5–15.

Mourelatos, A. P. D. (1978), 'Events, Processes and States', *Linguistics and Philosophy*, 2: 415–34.

——(1993), 'Aristotle's kinesis/energaia Distinction: A Marginal Note on Kathleen Gill's Paper', *Canadian Journal of Philosophy*, 23: 385–8.

Moya, C. (1990), *The Philosophy of Action* (Oxford).

Nagel, E. (1961), *The Structure of Science* (New York).

Nagel, E. (1977), 'Teleology Revisited', *Journal of Philosophy*, 84: 261–301.

Nagel, T. (1970), *The Possibility of Altruism* (Oxford).

——(1979), *Mortal Questions* (Cambridge).

Neander, K. (1991), 'Functions as Selected Effects: The Conceptual Analysts' Defense', *Philosophy of Science*, 58: 168–84.

Nozick, R. (1981), *Philosophical Explanations* (Cambridge, Mass.).

O'Shaughnessy, B. (1980), *The Will* (Cambridge).

Papineau, D. (1993), *Philosophical Naturalism* (Oxford).

Peacocke, C. (1979), *Holistic Explanation* (Oxford).

Pears, D. (1971), 'Ifs and Cans', *Canadian Journal of Philosophy*, 1: 249–74.

——(1984), *Motivated Irrationality* (Oxford).

Pitt, J. (1988) (ed.), *Theories of Explanation* (Oxford).

Putnam, H. (1981), *Reason, Truth and History* (Cambridge).

Railton, P. (1978), 'A Deductive-Nomological Model of Probabilistic Explanation', *Philosophy of Science*, 45: 206–26, repr. in Pitt (1988: 119–35).

Ramsey, F. (1978 edn.), *Foundations*, ed. D. Mellor (London).

Raz, J. (1978) (ed.), *Practical Reasoning* (Oxford).

Rescher, N. (1970), *Scientific Explanation* (New York).

Ruben, D.-H. (1993) (ed.), *Explanation* (Oxford).

Rumelhart, D., and McClelland, J. (1986), *Parallel Distributed Processing* (Cambridge, Mass.).

Russell, B. (1903), *The Principles of Mathematics* (London).

Ryle, G. (1949), *The Concept of Mind* (London).

Salmon, W. (1984), *Scientific Explanation and the Causal Structure of the World* (Princeton).

——(1989), 'Four Decades of Scientific Explanation', in Kitcher and Salmon (1989), 3–219.

——Jeffrey, R., and Greeno, J. (1971), *Statistical Explanation and Statistical Relevance* (Pittsburgh).

Sartre, J.-P. (1973 edn.), *Existentialism and Humanism* (London).

Scriven, M. (1959), 'Explanation and Prediction in Evolutionary Theory', *Science*, 130: 477–82.

Skinner, B. F. (1953), *Science and Human Behaviour* (New York).

Snowdon, P. (1981), 'Perception, Vision and Causation', *Proceedings of the Aristotelian Society*, 81: 175–92.

——(1990), 'The Objects of Perceptual Experience', *Proceedings of the Aristotelian Society*, suppl. vol. 64: 121–51.

Sober, E. (1984), *The Nature of Selection* (Cambridge, Mass.).

Sorabji, R. (1964), 'Function', *Philosophical Quarterly*, 14: 289–302.

Stoutland, F. (1982), 'Davidson, von Wright and the Debate over Causation', in Floistad (1982: 45–72).

——(1985), 'Davidson on Intentional Behaviour', in Lepore and McLaughlin (1985: 44–59).

Strawson, G. (1994), *Mental Reality* (Cambridge, Mass.).

Strawson, P. (1959), *Individuals* (London).

Taylor, C. (1964), *The Explanation of Behaviour* (London).

——(1977), 'What is Human Agency?', in T. Mischel (ed.), *The Self* (Oxford), 103–35, repr. in C. Taylor (1985: 15–44).

——(1985), *Philosophical Papers*, i. *Human Agency and Language* (Cambridge).

Taylor, R. (1966), *Action and Purpose* (Englewood Cliffs, NJ).

Thalberg, I. (1984), 'Do Our Intentions Cause Our Intentional Actions?', *American Philosophical Quarterly*, 21: 249–60.

van Fraassen, B. (1980), *The Scientific Image* (Oxford).

Vendler, Z. (1957), 'Verbs and Times', *Philosophical Review*, 66: 143–60.

Williams, B. (1981), *Moral Luck* (Cambridge).

Wittgenstein, L. (1958), *Philosophical Investigations* (Oxford).

——(1974 edn.), *Tractatus Logico-Philosophicus* (London).

Woodfield, A. (1976), *Teleology* (Cambridge).

Wright, G. H. von (1971), *Explanation and Understanding* (London).

Wright, L. (1973), 'Functions', *Philosophical Review*, 82: 139–68.

——(1976), *Teleological Explanation* (Berkeley and Los Angeles).

INDEX

Salmon, W. 40, 41 n., 51 n.
Sartre, J.-P. 21–3
satisfactoriness 135
sense 169
situational appreciation 133–7, 141–2,
    151, 166
Skinner, B. 99
Snowdon, P. 27
Sober, E. 111
sphexishness 112–22
Stoutland, F. 12, 14
Strawson, G. 175
Strawson, P. 48
subjectivity 143–50

Taylor, C. 14, 21–3, 94–5, 132
teleological explanation 6–14, 81–
    122
  internalist vs. externalist 11–14

Thalberg, I. 92
theoretical model, *see* method of
    deriving descriptions
thinking 140, 167–8

understanding 62–75

van Fraassen, B. 63

ways 96–8
weakness of will, *see* acrasia
Wiggins, D. 134
Williams, B. 35
Wittgenstein, L. 127
Woodfield, A. 82, 132
working assumptions 150–4, 164
von Wright, G. 12
Wright, L. 14, 87–8, 95, 100–5, 108–
    10, 164 n.